Beneath the Rain Shadow

Volume III

Stories, Poems, Essays

Whidbey Island, Washington

Copyright © 1999 by Whidbey Writers Group and individual authors

All rights reserved.
First edition.

LC Catalog Card No: 99-93727
ISBN: 0-7392-0173-5

The cover illustration by Olga Chambers shows Deception Pass Bridge, which connects Whidbey Island to Fidalgo Island off the coast of Washington State. Mount Baker is in the background.

Text illustrations by Jackie Griesinger and Olga Chambers.

Printed in the USA by

3212 East Highway 30 • Kearney, NE 68847 • 1-800-650-7888

Contents

Preface / *v*

The Whidbey Writers Group / *vii*

Bill Wilson
From Stowaway / 1
Keep Your Seventy-Three Cents / 12

Shalom Weizmann
Memories of My Schooldays / 14

Rama Weizmann
Normal / 28

Mariellen Houston Tissot
The Appraisal / 36
And It's Magic / 43
The Gloaming / 46
Evergreen / 46
Haight-Ashbury / 47
Lost Souls / 48

Jan Simpson
Shipping Out / 50

Sandra McGillivray Ortgies
Lanterns: An Island Mystery / 58
Ebey's Landing National Historical Reserve / 70
On a Scale of ... / 71
Time / 72
Flagger Ahead / 72

Jackie Griesinger
The Handicap   / 73
Geometry Lesson   / 77
The Scent of Lilacs   / 78
Point/Counterpoint   / 91

Helen Gleghorn
Jack   / 92

Suzanne Fulle
Legacy   / 95

Kaye LaTorra Erickson
Company's Coming   / 105
You Call This Progress?   / 107

Olga Chambers
The Little Mermaid's Awakening   / 108
My Summer Vacation   / 117

Murray Anderson
From Breederman   / 121

Ann Adams
The Secret Life of Paula Twitty   / 142
Best Friends   / 147

Preface

From all over the continent and as far away as Casablanca we came to live on Whidbey Island off the coast of Washington State. Every other Monday we meet to read and critique each other's work.

The Whidbey Writers Group started in 1990 with eight members. This Volume III of our published stories, poems, and essays includes pieces by the eleven of us who meet regularly, plus two members who have moved to California.

Jan Simpson, our newest member, wrote a poem about how the person who writes feels about the writer within:

She runs too fast,
jumps too high,
laughs too loud,
talks too much.
She hollers in the library,
mumbles at the table,
sings at funerals,
cries at parties.
She draws in the window frost
writes her name in the ledge dust,
dawdles in the shower,
fingers the soap bubbles.
She cartwheels in the kitchen,
shinnies up trees,
hop-scotches down the hall,
runs through the neighbor's hose
in her nice clothes.
She talks with her mouth full,
licks the bowl,
takes the last cookie,
wipes her mouth on her sleeve.

She stares at the handicapped,
    talks to strangers,
        belches in fine company,
            won't eat her brussels sprouts.
She asks the wrong questions,
    like "what's sclerosis of the liver?"
        says the wrong things,
            like "Gee, the bride looks fat!"
                thinks about too many things
                    that don't fit in the box.
She leaves her scribblings here and there,
    streaks of colored lights and rainbows,
        bits of ribbon, wooden beads,
            string and licorice mixed with pebbles,
                squibs of mud and paste.
I check the grammer,
    fix the spelling,
        mark it up from top to bottom,
            change the words around.
Then we talk about marketing,
    and I try to explain
        why it doesn't meet the rules,
            why it just won't work,
                why it's too too-too,
                    why it's not too-too enough.
And she shrugs as if to say okay,
    and I think she's understood.
        So I change it round and round some more,
            Until she says, "You've killed it."
Then I lose my temper
    and she scampers away,
        and I feel fairly smug,
            like I've sent her to her room,
                only to find she's taken the light with her.

The Whidbey Writers Group

Ann Adams moved from Texas to Whidbey Island with her husband Mark in 1982. They built Packrat Press in Oak Harbor and printed and published books until Mark's death in 1997. Ann has wanted to be a writer since she first came to consciousness, and she has wanted to write a Walter Mitty story since she first read the original in high school in 1953. She took her first writing class at the University of Oklahoma in Norman in 1968. After attending Bill Skubi's and Marian Blue's classes on Whidbey Island in the mid-'90s, she enrolled in the novel writing course at the University of Washington in 1997. She is working on her first novel.

Murray Anderson was born on Whidbey Island, where he has retired with his wife of forty-seven years. He has a bachelor of science degree in Dairy Husbandry from Washington State University. His first professions were as a dairyman, herdsman, milking machine salesman, artificial inseminator, and fieldman for an artificial insemination cooperative. Before retirement he was CEO of several nonprofit human service agencies. His poetry and short stories have been published in a variety of literary magazines. He recently finished *Breederman,* a novel about the demise of the family farm and its impact on the lives of farm families, and is looking for a publisher. The excerpt in this collection is from this novel.

Olga Chambers. Before all other pleasures, reading is Olga's favorite pastime. She has dabbled in other hobbies, among them photography, painting, and serigraphy: the cover of this book is one of her paintings. Writing for pleasure is a recent interest, one that Olga started upon her retirement. It is with the support and the encouragement of the writers' group and the senior classes offered through the Skagit Valley College Extension that she has been able to draw upon past experiences to create the fiction she writes.

vii

Kaye La Torra Erickson lives on the beach at Long Point near Coupeville on Whidbey Island with her husband Harvey. Having retired from nursing at Whidbey General Hospital, she has written articles for local newspapers on medical topics of interest to retired persons, and articles for technical publications. A charter member of the Whidbey Writers, she has recently turned her attention to fiction writing, primarily short short stories.

Suzanne Fulle was born and raised in Houston, Texas, graduated from Rice University, and attended Columbia Teacher's College in New York City, where she studied with Pearl Buck. She married Floyd Fulle, attorney at law, and moved to Seattle, where she published *Lanterns for Fiesta*, a novel about a Mexican family in Houston. She is working on a historical novel based on the life of her great-great-great-great-grandparents of North Carolina, Tennessee, and Louisiana during and after the American Revolution. She has three grown children and a gorgeous granddaughter in Japan.

Helen Gleghorn was born Helen Aileen Leake in Tulsa, Oklahoma, on July 18, 1920. After graduating from high school, she left Tulsa to be married in Glendale, California, in 1941 to William Goldy Gleghorn. They had four children: Bill, Judy, Diane, and Carol. Helen was a campfire leader for seven years, and was awarded a National Honor from Camp Fire Girls for being a creative leader. She lived in California from 1942 to 1977, then came to Whidbey Island in December of 1977 with her husband. In March 1987, she became a widow after forty-five years of marriage. She started writing her life story for her children, her eight grandchildren, and nine great-grandchildren.

Jackie Griesinger was born in a small town in Iowa and moved to California a few months after Pearl Harbor. When she and her husband retired to Whidbey Island, she was able to pursue many hobbies that had been on hold for a long time. She says, "I get so many ideas for plots, story lines, and poetry, it drives me crazy that I can't get them all down and printed out." "The Handicap" is a true story about four men who played golf one day in September of 1994. Lou, Jackie's husband, who made the hole-in-one, is legally blind. About the other pieces in this collection she says, "'The Scent of Lilacs' has been brewing in my head for at least two years, and 'Geometry Lesson' is a poem that seems to affect everybody differently. Who makes up the triangle? You decide."

Sandra McGillivray Ortgies, a Canadian, lived by the sea in West Vancouver, B.C., her first 22 years. Wanting a change and realizing there wasn't anywhere more beautiful in Canada than the Vancouver area, she moved to San Francisco in 1964, where she met Don and joined in on the Air Force Adventure. Their son Ross was born in 1970, and AF tours in San Antonio, Texas, central Germany, and Illinois followed. Sandra finally pulled together the courses attended at eight colleges to achieve a degree in Psychology from Texas Lutheran College. After retiring from the AF in 1992, the Ortgies made an inspired move to a cottage on the beach at the south end of Whidbey Island, where Sandra pursued her interest in writing by taking a series of classes with writer/editor Marian Blue and attending University of Washington writing workshops. After four years on Mutiny Bay, and true to their AF inner clock, the Ortgies moved, but only 20 miles up-island to the historic town of Coupeville and a home overlooking Penn Cove. Sandra is presently writing articles, short stories, and poems, as well as consigning antiques and collectibles with Penn Cove Antique Mall and being a host/member of the Military Bed & Breakfast association, "Retreat & Reveille." Her essay in this volume, "Ebey's Landing Historical Reserve," best describes her appreciation of living on Whidbey Island.

Jan Simpson was born in Calgary, Canada, in 1953. She graduated from the University of Calgary in Economics and went on to become a Chartered Accountant. She met her Texan husband Jim on her first attempt to move to Seattle. Sidetracked to Houston, she pursued her interest in computers, working as a senior systems analyst and database administrator for an oil and gas company, then left work to have and raise her only son, Alex. In 1997, the family made a second, this time successful, attempt to move to the Rain Shadow, choosing Whidbey Island as home. When Jan's not keeping books and designing a website for her husband's automotive design and development studio, or playing Mom to six-year-old Alex, she dabbles in writing. Or you can find her walking one of Whidbey's beaches or watching the ferry shuttle across the Sound from her favorite perch at Fort Casey.

Mariellen Houston Tissot has lived on and off Whidbey Island for the past fifty-five years. Houston Road, near the center of the island, is named for her pioneering grandfather, who arrived here in the early 1920s. Mariellen now lives on South Whidbey, on Sweetwater Farm, with her husband Jeremiah and a variety of four-legged friends. She spends her time writing, gardening, selling real estate, and operating Sweetwater Cottage, a bed and breakfast.

Rama Weizmann was born in Brooklyn, New York, to Russian and Polish Jewish immigrant parents. Family legend associates Rama's birth on October 15, 1929, with the stock market crash and the Day of Atonement, Jewish Yom-Kippur. Myriad cultural chemicals melded to produce her avidly curious, adventurous personality: *Dick and Jane*, the 1930's Depression, the American pioneering spirit, World War II, and the Holocaust. Following retirement from a dedicated, fulfilling career as a social worker and psychotherapist, she and her husband Shalom moved to lovely Oak Harbor, Washington, where she decided to explore interests which had lain dormant for years. This was the beginning of her experiments with short story writing, quilting, gardening, and exploring nature. She and her husband moved recently to California to be closer to their family. She hopes children and grandchildren will be interested in her writing.

Shalom Weizmann was born December 22, 1923, in Casablanca, Morocco, during the French Colonial era. The son of a large poor Jewish family, he grew up in the Mellah (ghetto) within its medieval and narrow streets. He spent his youth enjoying the sunny beaches of the Atlantic. After the landing of the U.S. Army in North Africa in World War II, he volunteered to join the Free French Army and chased the Nazis from the French Riviera to the heart of the German Fatherland. The year 1948 found him in the ranks of the young Israeli Army fighting for the survival of the new state of Israel. Following the Six Day war of 1967, he immigrated with his family to the United States, where he went back to school and became a computer systems analyst. In 1988, he retired and migrated with his wife Rama to the quiet and beautiful sounds of the Northwest. They moved recently to Coastal California to be close to their family. Shalom decided to write about his life experiences in order to share them with his six children and eight grandchildren.

Bill Wilson was born in Orlando, Florida, in 1944 — long before Disney World — and grew up in a middle-class family in Florida and Georgia before graduating from Auburn University and joining the Air Force. Spending most of his Air Force career on the North Dakota, Montana, and Nebraska plains, he and his wife Myrna spent countless winter weekends following their only son, Greg, from hockey rink to hockey rink throughout the northern United States and southern Canada. After retiring from the Air Force in 1988, he completed a journalism degree at the University of Nebraska at Omaha. He then moved to Whidbey Island, having discovered this little paradise some fifteen years before. He worked as a reporter for *Whidbey News-Times* for three years and is now a freelance writer, contributing primarily to the *Whidbey Reporter*, which he helped found (as the *Coupeville Examiner*) in 1995.

Bill Wilson

From Stowaway

The fourth of three souls aboard U.N. Tug *Allie Marie* soon bound for Mars, I come looking for a story — or perhaps to beget one. But that may prove a tough task because . . . Well because I don't seem to have any hands to write with or even a voice to record. I'm just not all here.

No. No, that didn't sound quite right. I am perfectly sane. I mean I just found myself inside this complete stranger's head, looking through his eyes — seeing what he sees, smelling what he smells, feeling what he touches, tasting what he tastes. Speaking of which, he just took a drink from a some kind of collapsible bladder. Tastes like . . . Well, I can't exactly place it: some cross between Gatoraid and gasoline. Hope this doesn't presage the rest of the menu.

Every writer knows you need to get inside your character's mind, but this approach is a bit too literal for my taste. Besides, I don't seem to have any control over his body, which waxes a mite inconvenient, having left my own body in some other place, some other time. But I can read his thoughts, at least some of them. That's how I know he's mission navigator George Cedenyo and that this space tug will be towing a supply pod — a kind of interplanetary barge — to resupply a Martian research outpost. Far as I can tell, George doesn't realize I'm sharing his brain as we watch a row of amber lights sequence on and off across a gray-green panel in front of us.

Guess I must sound pretty blase for someone in my predicament. I wasn't this way a few minutes ago when I first realized what happened to me. I felt all the panic of a bungee jumper whose cord just snapped above a craggy

Beneath the Rain Shadow

canyon. But how does a disembodied mind manifest panic. It can't call 9-1-1. It can't scream or cry or puke or even roll into the fetal position. After visualizing all those conditioned responses in the silent movie of my mind, I soon grasped the futility and began to calmly assess. So now it's just real strange, like I'm me and George at the same time.

So who am I, and how did I get here? Well, I'm Jack — Jack Jenkins, that is — and I'm not exactly sure how I got here. I remember staring at a blinking cursor, trying to write a Sunday magazine feature about a Puget Sound fisherman struggling to cope with sparse salmon runs and abundant government restrictions. That couldn't have been more than a half hour or so ago: around five in the afternoon on April 19, 1998. Guess you could say I swam up the wrong spawning stream. When I couldn't conjure just the right metaphor to peg the *Ellie May*, my fisherman's barnacle-scarred boat, I decided to play a game or two of computer solitaire. My first inkling of anything amiss came when I absentmindedly dragged the Jack of diamonds onto the Queen of Hearts. Instead of rudely bouncing the card back onto the stack the way it normally does, the computer left the card where I put it: red on red.

Puzzled by the program's behavior, I tried to reach for the keyboard to launch my virus checker. That's when I started feeling a bit lightheaded, like the blood all rushed from my head to my ass. Next the solitaire cards disappeared, and the monitor turned black with row after row of orange characters I couldn't make out — like a spontaneous cut-and-paste. Guess I was the one cut and pasted. Like my own computer monitor, the lower right corner of the screen still showed April 19, but the year — the year read 2069. That's all. It was nothing like being beamed up or anything, no white lights or swirling tunnels — not even a fall down a rabbit hole. I don't own any kind of talisman, not even a Salish dream catcher. The coiled cobra spring of time must have wound itself too tight around me and relieved its tension, catapulting me seventy-three years ahead, not to mention 500 miles into space. When I tried to rub my eyes or slap myself, I realized I had no hands of my own, and I was seeing through someone else's eyes. Like I said before, that's when I tried to panic, but failed.

I know what you're thinking. He's dreaming — or hallucinating. That's what I thought too at first. Maybe that's the real reason my panic subsided and I began to notice how . . . well how normal everything seemed — other than my phantom status, that is. My past dreams always seemed blurry and disjointed, like the other night I dreamed I was being pursued by a mutant black-and-white orangutan through Alderwood Mall. I couldn't make out whether I was passing the Bon or J C Penney because all the stores looked like watercolors painted by a five-year-old. Then while sprinting past a pastel blur that might have been Orange Julius, I suddenly found myself sitting at the breakfast table as a schoolboy asking my mother to pass the sugar.

Not that I spend much time on twenty-first century spaceships, but this setting is nothing like that or any dreamscape I recall. It just seems so tactile, so ordinary. We're in a cylindrical compartment about fifteen feet long with a ten-foot diameter. Another console similar to George's rests about three feet forward of his along the same bulkhead. A man in royal blue coveralls is sitting there with his head buried in the pages of a thick loose-leaf binder. A third, unmanned console sits beneath an oval viewport at the forward end of the compartment. The consoles, along with about a dozen four-foot-high electronic racks, are mounted on a charcoal-gray grated metal floor. Each console has a padded high-back chair covered with a blue serge fabric of some kind and mounted on short rails for sliding to nearby electronic racks. I see every rivet in the baby-shit green bulkhead. I hear no echos in the voices. And except for my trip from the past, time appears quite linear. I've watched second by second while nearly forty-five minutes have ticked off the computer chronometer.

Beneath the Rain Shadow

No, this is not like any dream I've experienced. And, by the way, I don't do drugs.

"OK, George, ready for the pre-launch checklist whenever you are."

That was first officer and co-pilot, Lt. Cmdr. Martin Jones, the Teutonic-looking guy seated at the adjacent console. He has a blond crew cut and angular cheek bones. If he wasn't so short, about five-six I'd say, he could have posed as poster boy for Hitler's master race. George considers him a pain in the ass because of his by-the-book military approach to hauling cargo across space — not to mention the irritating way he sucks air through his teeth. George ignores him.

"Cedenyo," Jones repeats, more insistent. "I said I was ready. . ."

"I heard you," George interrupts. Our voice bears a hint of Hispanic accent and more than a hint of sarcasm. "I will let you know when I'm ready, man."

Me again, still pondering my quandary. If I am dreaming after all, why can't I wake up. Nearly an hour has passed. Dreams are only supposed to last a few minutes, aren't they? And what would have put this notion in my head anyway? Never was much into science fiction. Oh, I read my share as a kid, I guess. Still faithfully watch each succeeding Star Trek generation, and I saw all the Star Wars movies like most everybody. But I never went to any of those conventions made up like a Klingon, or anything like that.

I don't know what's going on, but I'm not making it up. Besides, if I was going to dream myself into the future, why pick a flying tug boat on a routine supply mission less than 100 years from now. I mean from then . . . Whatever. No one has invented warp drive yet, so it will take months to get to Mars. They haven't met up with any Klingons or even pointy-eared Vulcans. I can't even hear a Strauss waltz accompanying our spin around the Earth — just the dull drone of fans cooling the electronic racks. You can find more exciting stuff in tabloid headlines. I can almost see it in the Safeway check-out line on the rack above the Butterfingers and Juicy Fruit gum: WRITER RETURNS FROM FUTURE SPACE FLIGHT, FINDS ELVIS RUNNING DISCO ON DARK SIDE OF MOON. Just had another disturbing thought. What if this guy George is schizophrenic, and I'm just his other self? That would mean I never existed outside of his mind, and his imagination fabricated my whole twentieth-century life. Is that how it works? Recalling psychology 101 and *The Three Faces of Eve*, I think only one personality or another in a schizophrenic can be active at a time. If I were his other self being aware like I am, wouldn't I just take over? So far I'm just a passive observer. I can "listen" to what he's thinking now, but I only seem able to research specific questions in his memory — kind of like when you query a computer database. No, I must be a separate entity. Decartes was right. Body or no body, Cogito ergo sum.

But then there's this annoying time travel thing. As enticing as moving backward and forward in time might sound, I still can't quite buy it. I know this sounds like an odd pronouncement given my present circumstance. Maybe I'm long dead, and my consciousness somehow survived to land in this future man's mind, sort of like that woman in Yelm, Washington, who claimed an ancient warrior periodically took over her mind. "There are more things in heaven and earth, Horatio . . ." I'm trying to stay calm, but I really am starting to feel like the man in the iron mask. At least he could scream.

Oblivious of my musings, George continues entering and verifying course parameters for this pre-mission test flight around the moon to check out *Allie Marie's* new high-efficiency ion engines. The retrofit vessel just completed space trials by Boeing engineers, but now must complete a final test with her regular crew. She doesn't actually leave on the next supply mission until Earth and Mars are more favorably aligned in about three weeks. Once the engines prove their reliability, the launch and return windows will open much wider and more often.

I sense George feeling puzzled and suspicious about this test flight. They already took her on a two-week shakedown, and unmanned missions using the new engine have already made the Mars trip without a hitch. In this little jaunt around the moon, the ion engines will add almost nothing to our speed. And flight crew procedures are virtually unchanged. So why this extra test flight? He's convinced the higher-ups aren't telling us everything about this sortie.

"What you think about the extra test flight?" George asks Martin.

"What about it?"

"Don't you think it's kinda curious? Has to be a last-minute thing, or they wouldn't have called us off leave early. And I doubt it has much to do with the new engines, else they wouldn't give us the ship back. At least not without contractors coming along."

"Those decisions are above our pay grade. . . Let's just do our job like professionals. Which reminds me. Didn't you have time for a haircut before reporting in?"

"Give it a rest, Commander. I'm within regs." George pushes his black bangs out of our eyes and resumes entering course data.

When it does go, this will be George's sixth Mars mission — this time to deliver supplies to outpost Zeta 3, near the red planet's south pole. For George, the trip has long since become robotic, even though he's in cold sleep all but three days of the trip. Once there he doesn't even get to visit the surface of the planet. They orbit, release the barge to land on its own, then refuel and spend some R&R time on Phobos — one of two Martian moons. In our mind he isn't needed; a computer does all the real navigation. In fact, they don't really need a crew at all. The only reason they man these supply missions is to make sure they have enough trained flight crews for moving people to future colonies and for exploring the outer planets. So if this is such a routine thing, where's the story? Is there really some metaphysical purpose in my being here? And when George sleeps, what happens to me? Me with no body, at least not in this century. Even the wonders of the universe could get old for a rookie space traveler all alone. But not yet. Right now I feel like a moth just breaking out of its cocoon.

From the corner of our eye, out the porthole beside his console, I see Puget Sound some 500 miles below looking like one of those relief map posters you see in roadside tourist traps. Can't quite pick out the Stillaguamish, the Skykomish or any of the "ish" rivers burrowing their way out of the Cascade and Olympic Mountains down to the sound. Wonder if any salmon have survived to spawn in those rivers. Wonder if any fir or cedar still stand along their banks. If George knows, it's buried too deep in his memory for me to find.

Normally he wouldn't notice the silent flash from the parking thrusters on a shuttle docking at an adjacent arm on Unity 7 Spaceport. But this time he looks up from the checklist. Wonder why? Because of me? I know I can't control his body, but what about his mind? Did my curiosity convince him to look out the porthole? Let's try something.

George, scratch your left earlobe.

A finger twitches, and he wonders what caused it, but makes no move for the ear. Some reaction though; I must be something more than just a parasite. We continue to gaze at the earth below.

Against the white clouds hovering over the Olympic Mountains, the hydrazine plume from that shuttle springs like green onions from an April garden. Never mind the surreal silence, void of cricket chirps or whirr of hummingbird wings. In my century, such a scene would cry out for orchestral accompaniment or at least a TV commercial for Trans Lunar Airlines or maybe some fat-free margarine.

"What am I doing?" George mumbles to himself. "I don't have time to stare out the window."

My erstwhile orchestra silent, George returns to his pre-mission checklist.

"OK, read your silly checklist."

"What was that?" asks Martin, apparently pretending not

to hear.

"You heard me, asshole," George retorts. I feel our lips curl into a smile.

The U.N. Space Command is a quasi-military organization, or at least that's how George's memory characterizes it, and Jones outranks him. But George knows just how much insubordination he can get away with — especially with Jones. He's all spit and polish, and he tosses orders at George like a musher to a dog team. But when it comes to enforcing his edicts, he usually misplaces his balls. Besides, there just aren't that many qualified navigators around. So George doesn't shrink from a little cheek here and there.

"We'll just assume I didn't hear that, Lieutenant," says Martin, forcing his voice to a lower pitch. "I'm on page Mike two four. . . Insertion time equals zero zero one three Zulu."

"Entered and verified," George answers almost like one of those computer voice simulations they use to tell you your bank balance or that someone's phone number has changed.

"Launch azimuth equals two seven four degrees, thirty-three minutes."

"Yeah, yeah. Got it," George responds while depressing three switch-indicators to the right of his computer display. The switches blink rapidly for a few seconds then glow steady green. Guess the flight computer takes course parameters by voice recognition, since neither crewman is typing them in.

"A simple 'check' will suffice," says Martin.

"A half-trained orangutan could do this job," he mutters.

Hmm. Could this be conflict? May find a story here yet. Or maybe not. George appears to be parrying in a duel of wits with an unarmed opponent.

"The skipper's not going to put up with your attitude for long," Jones responds.

Ah yes, the skipper. Martin doesn't know the half of it. The beautiful, iron-willed Commander Milloy would not tolerate such from George or anyone else in her command. He would be about as likely to mock her as an Egyptian slave refusing to fan Nefertiti. But Martin doesn't know her the way George does. Jones has only been assigned to her crew for the past two months. This will be his first mission under her command. Ambitious. Yes. Hard-nosed. Yes. But somehow George knows she would go to the wall for a loyal crew member. He would fly into the sun for her.

I'm trying to probe his mind for what sparked such loyalty when the airlock into the crew compartment hisses like a punctured tire. Red notebook in hand, mission commander Sharon Milloy stoops through the four-foot door in the bulkhead leading from the airlock. The spinning space station lends a slight artificial gravity to the tug, so she is not completely weightless. But at only about one-quarter her 120 or so earth pounds, she covers the dozen feet to the command console in two antelope strides. Her light chestnut hair winds up in a swirl under a gray plastic headset; any features of her body remain well hidden beneath loose-fitting, royal-blue coveralls. In case anyone wonders how I decided her hair was chestnut instead of auburn or just plain brown, I remember it from a box of hair color in the drug store I saw a few days ago while waiting for my wife to decide on what shade of lipstick she needed.

George fixes on a stray curl nearly surrounding a freckle beside her ear. She meets our gaze with a look I'd call surprise, then the slightest hint of a smile. She quickly looks away. As do we. What's this? Familiarity? Wishful thinking? Can't quite make out George's feelings here: some juxtaposition of lust on disgust. No hint of chauvinism though. Women must have finally conquered that — at least in George Cedenyo's mind. As for me, the feelings are pretty much all lust. Baggy flight suit or not, this is one fine looking woman. Helen of Troy would surely have paled beside her. But still just minutes out of the twentieth century, I can't help wondering how she handles the pressures of command. Her face probably could launch a thousand ships, but I don't know about leading them into battle or across the solar system.

"How goes it, Skipper?" Martin asks. "Can't wait to get going on this one."

Here comes the ass-kissing already, we think. Though it doesn't sound like such a bad idea to me.

Without a responding platitude, the brown-eyed skipper opens her bomb bay doors and releases the ordnance on her unsuspecting crew and her stowaway too.

"OK, guys, I'll get right to it," she says in a subdued but distinct Aussie accent. As she props her right foot on a rung of her rail-mounted chair, her countenance bears an expression she could have borrowed from General Patton just before he engaged one of Rommel's panzer divisions — like one wanting to convey the weight of the mission, and to wish the men Godspeed because they may well be dead by sunset; but the excitement and sense of history and self-importance wax so great, the eyes bounce like a kid about to ride her first roller coaster.

"We're not going to Zeta 3 after all. We're going to Cydonia. . . They found something there." She pulls a handkerchief in from an open zipper pocket in the leg of her flight suit and wipes the beading perspiration from her forehead.

Cydonia? Isn't that where that probe in the '70s photographed the face on Mars? I know what she's talking about — without relying on George. I came across a web site about it on the Internet a few months ago, or was it decades ago? A rock formation photographed in the 1970s by a NASA probe. It looked like a huge stone face peering out into space. NASA dismissed it as a trick of light and shadow — a natural formation that just looked sort of like a face from that angle at that time of day. They ridiculed anyone who thought otherwise, saying it was no different from seeing a cloud that looked like an alligator or rocks on a cliff that looked like John Kennedy or the Virgin Mary.

The lunatic fringe had a field day — insisting the face was built by the same ancient astronauts who built the

Sphinx in Egypt. That's why many legitimate scientists kept a low profile, not wanting to be lumped with the cuckoo birds. But if I recall right, certain aspects of the face made it more intriguing than the average cloud formation. For one, it still looked like a face from two different angles. There were even computer enhanced images seeming to show eyes and teeth – even a teardrop. Not only that, but other formations in the vicinity looked curiously symmetrical, especially a number of pyramid-like formations.

But this whole thing should have been resolved within a couple of decades after I left. They've apparently had manned outposts on Mars since the 2020s, and they're just now checking this out?

Can't seem to get past George's present thoughts to find the answer. Guess his emotional state has closed down my access to his memory. He seems stunned. I feel his heart race as his stomach churns the chili he had for lunch. Guess they do eat some real food in space.

"As of now, no more voice communications outside the ship," Milloy continues. "This is no test flight. We launch for Mars at 2215 Zulu: that gives us about an hour and forty-five minutes."

"But, Skipper," Martin pleads. "The window doesn't open for six weeks! The computer won't even compute the orbit till then."

"Haven't you heard?" Destiny still dances in her voice. "With these new engines, we can leave just about anytime. With the updated velocity vectors, I think you'll find the computer will spit out the new course quicker than a dingo'll down a lost lamb."

"But what about my wife?" Martin is almost whining. "I have to call her. We're supposed to go to San Francisco the week before we were going to leave."

"You can send her e-mail," she replied coldly. "But I have to screen it for classified. . . Just tell her the mission got moved up. Sorry."

"With all due respect, ma'am, what's really going on

here?" George asks. "What do you mean they found something?"

"Heard something actually. Can't tell you any more until after we launch," she says, apparently now able to throttle her excitement. "The official reason for the early departure is that Zeta 3 needs an emergency parts delivery. . . Input the new time and target, and get going on the rest of the pre flight. We don't have much time."

Martin stares dumfounded and stoop shouldered; his military bearing is gone. George must be wearing a like expression. His mind projects a rapid-fire collage of images mostly too jumbled for me to fix on: his mother in Las Cruces — but no image of a father — a small black dog, a bed of strawberries, a billowing red-and-yellow spinnaker, a slender young man wearing faded jeans and an olive-drab T-shirt . . .

"I said get to it!" Milloy bellows, sounding more like a bull gorilla than a beauty queen.

Forget what I said about her leadership qualities. *When do we charge that hill ma'am?*

Author's note: This story began as an experiment with point of view. Every writer wants to get inside the head of his character. So I thought it would be fun to literally put a writer inside the head of another character.

Keep Your 73 Cents

Just wanted a sandwich and some fries to nourish my mate-led mall trek. I know. I know I should pass up the fries with all that fat and salt. But the salt ended up in the wound I wasn't ready for. I didn't ask for any special favors. No affirmative action for me.

All the same, the skinny blond girl

behind the food-court cash register – who must have been all of sixteen — slashes me with the unkindest cut when she turns to her supervisor and says,

"How much is senior discount?"

"Ten percent," comes the reply over the sizzle of meat on the grill.

I turn around to look behind me. She must be looking ahead to the shriveled bald guy in line behind me, the one who looks like he died the week before. I'm still a svelte fifty-four — far too young for a senior discount. Sure my hair's prematurely gray, and I have a stiff back from time to time, but a senior discount? I ski and hike and lift weights. I'm still trying to decide what to be when I grow up, for crying out loud.

"That'll be $7.14 with your 73-cent discount," she says with callous brutality. "Your order number is 343."

Stunned, I took the change from my $10 bill and slouched toward a lavender plastic table — close to the trash can with the hinged lid, but far too far from Bethlehem — while my wife waited for the food.

"Keep your 73 cents," I wanted to say. But I didn't. Just gummed the sandwich and fries, and burped my way closer to oblivion.

Shalom Weizmann

Memories of My Schooldays

I was three years old in 1927 when I began attending the Heder Synagogue, Sunday through Friday. The Heder, a rectangular, large store front, was in a cul-de-sac, Mattress Street, in the *mellah* of Casablanca.

It had a high ceiling, rugged walls painted with white limestone, and an uneven concrete floor splintered in several places. There were no windows, and the only light permeating the inside darkness entered through the open wide wooden door.

Rough unfinished wooden benches faced a small closet where the three Torah scrolls were housed. The closet was covered by a hand-embroidered heavy curtain. Four heavy wooden beams criss-crossed the ceiling and supported private dwellings above the synagogue. Two big copper oil lamps suspended from the support beams completed the austere decorum.

The synagogue was a learning location for boys, and in addition, three daily Jewish prayers took place inside it. The students took part in the afternoon prayer because we arrived after the morning prayer and left before the evening one. The Rabbi, financially secure, assumed the functions of cantor, teacher and educator. He collected a nominal small weekly fee from those who could afford it.

No sanitation was provided, and boys in need of urinating simply went outside and peed in a bucket standing against the corner street wall adjacent to the synagogue. Boys in need of a water closet were sent to their respective homes. I often used that excuse to leave the Heder and go home for a while, whereas some boys left and did not return for the day. We drank water from a huge clay jar, using a tin can nailed to a stick of wood. It defied all hygienic standards.

There were two levels of learning. One was for

Shalom Weizmann 15

beginners, who were taught the Hebrew alphabet. The advanced level learned the daily and festival prayers and studied the weekly Torah portion. We also read some of the attached commentaries. On Wednesday we read the prophets and listened to our Rabbi's interpretation. None of the boys understood what was read in Hebrew, but we all memorized the chanting and the rules attached to the portion of the prayers.

A group of six or seven boys shared one book. One boy sat and held the book flat on his lap while the small group formed a circle around him. We read in unison and rapidly acquired the ability to read Hebrew upside-down and sideways. By the age of five I had mastered the reading of the prayers and the chanting of the Torah. I often accompanied my father to the Sabbath morning prayer in our neighborhood synagogue and sometimes I read a portion of the Torah to the joy and pride of my father.

When the Rabbi had to absent himself for a short while, he designated me to carry on with the reading while an older boy was appointed to keep order. But when the Rabbi had to plead the case of a husband or wife at the local Jewish tribunal for marriages and divorces, his youngest son Haim showed up at the synagogue to supervise the flock.

He was a teenager with an ugly face who enjoyed terrorizing us. Once when his father was away, Haim appointed two boys to stand at the door, keep a watch and alert him if somebody was coming toward the synagogue. In a dark corner of the Heder, he ordered a small group of boys to surround him, shut up, and listen to his stories. He asked one of the boys: "Do you know what we boys have inside our pants?"

Without hesitation the boy answered: "I knowww! The thing I make peepee with."

"You are stupid like a donkey. Listen to me or I'll slap your face."

An eerie silence followed. We were scared and fascinated at the same time. I seized the occasion and cut the silence by appealing to Haim: "Please do not get mad at us. We are young and we do not know these tricks. If you beat up anyone, I'll scream and run away."

My threat had an effect on him and calmed his anger. He then said: "Fine. I'll show you. But keep your mouths shut." He was about to unbutton his pants and pull out his penis when the watch guards shrieked in despair: "Haim, Haim! The Rabbi and another man are coming!"

Haim hastily buttoned his pants and with a threatening voice he ordered: "Go back to your seats and do not say a word to nobody." We returned to our seats, grabbed the books and resumed reading.

The following morning one of the boys came to the Heder accompanied by his mother. She was a corpulent young well-to-do woman, judging by her attire. She faced the Rabbi and with an angry voice told him the following story: "Yesterday we sat down for dinner and my son told his father in front of his older sister: 'Abba! Abba! This afternoon I learned how to play with my penis.'"

"Needless to say," the mother continued, "we wanted to know how and where my son learned those such things. So I asked him: 'You must have learned it in the synagogue. Who told you?' My son began crying. But my husband, insisted that he tells us the whole story, and so my little boy told us that yesterday during your absence, he participated in this disgrace. How could things like this happen inside this sacred synagogue? I'm very upset that my son has to ask me questions about his male organ in front of his sister. It is shameful, it is shameful!"

Before the Rabbi had a chance to ask her for some clarifications, she continued her tirade and wagging her left index finger at Haim, who was standing close to his father, she indignantly yelled: "This miserable son of yours is sullying this place of worship. He showed his private parts to my son and other kids in front of the Torah scrolls."

She was incensed about the act but much more concerned about the sanctity of the place than the sexual deed, since sex is usually talked about openly in the Moroccan culture.

Shalom Weizmann

The Rabbi, astounded by her accusations, grabbed his son by the neck and ordered him: "Tell me the truth. Did you do what this boy and his mother are accusing you of?"

"No. No. I did not do such a thing. I swear, I swear," Haim answered with a timid voice.

The woman ignored Haim's denial and, determined to win, she continued by addressing the Rabbi with her acerbic tone of voice: "Ask any of these boys, and you will find out who is telling the truth. My son tells me the truth, always."

The Rabbi looked around him and yelled my name: "Shalom! Where are you?"

I was seated on a corner of a bench hiding behind another boy. The Rabbi finally located me and, pointing his right index finger at me, intoned: "Shalom, come close and tell me what happened here yesterday during my absence."

I closed my eyes, trying to dispel the bloody image of my face smashed by an angry Haim, and with a quivering voice, I said: "Yesterday Haim played with his..." I could not pronounce the word penis in front of the Rabbi.

Fatherly, he encouraged me: "Continue, continue."

I pointed at my zipper and exclaimed: "He wanted to play with his.... in front of us."

The woman, victorious, chanted: "Didn't I tell you! My son tells me the truth, always. If Haim stays here, I will take my son to another Heder."

She made the following pledge: "I will make a big lunch of couscous for the children and pray to God to forgive us all from profaning this consecrated place."

The humiliated Rabbi promised her: "Haim will be punished, and never will he step inside this synagogue."

Facing his son, he slapped him twice, armed himself with his leather whip and began lashing his son on his bottom. Haim screamed from pain and repeated: "I will never do it again. I promise. I promise."

The tears and pain of his son awakened the Rabbi's pity and he stopped the punishment.

Before he sent his son home, he cursed him in Hebrew for shaming his name. This ended the scandal.

A week later, around noon, the woman came to the synagogue followed by three Arab porters carrying on their heads enormous wooden receptacles containing steaming couscous and other foods. We all ate, and after the meal the Rabbi blessed her and thanked her. That day we did not go home for lunch, and our panicky mothers showed up at the synagogue to inquire what happened.

When I reached the age of six, my mother decided it was time for me to go to the Alliance Israelite school and learn French. The task of registering a Jewish child to one of the two Alliance primary schools was not easy. They could not accommodate thousands of Jewish children who wished to join the students' ranks. For every available seat in school there were five or six candidates. Economic hard times, despair and hunger attracted Jews from southern villages and towns to the big city in search of jobs, food and shelter. This resulted in a rapid increase of the Jewish population of Casablanca.

Mothers accompanied by their children, sometimes more than one, spent days waiting in long lines trying to register their children for the coming school year. For two long days my mother and I stood in line under the punishing July sun and never got close to the school gate. She felt powerless and angry at the situation. Temporarily, she had to give up because my other brothers and sisters demanded her care and attention. Faced with another year of going to the Heder, I told her: "You know, Mamma. I will not go back to the Heder. I already know all the prayers by heart."

She dismissed my threat with her wide smile, held my hand and said: "I will ask my cousin to take care of your registration, and I'm sure she will succeed."

We got back home, and after she cooked dinner she went to see Soulikah, her childless cousin, who lived in a new neighborhood, outside the ghetto. Soulikah had acquired Portuguese citizenship through her husband, Mr. Benzaken, a successful businessman. My mother was her

Shalom Weizmann 19

confidante, and Soulikah adored me. In comparison to the majority of Moroccan Jewish women of that epoch Soulikah, an attractive woman, acted like a cultured lady. Her stay in Lisbon with her husband taught her the ways of the rich and sophisticated. She was always elegantly dressed, and her clothes attested to her status. She spoke French fluently, and in colonial French Morocco she was considered a European with special rights, in contrast to the masses of destitute Moroccan Jews.

A few days following my mother's failure, Soulikah came home and took me to school to be registered for the coming school year. On our way she instructed me: "Shalom! If you are asked what is our family relationship, you say that you are my nephew, and your mother, my sister, is dead."

At hearing that my mother was dead, I choked on my tears. Sensing my grief she admonished me: "Do not cry! It is pretending, pretending. You understand, young man."

The streets of the *mellah* were cobblestoned with wide gaps in between. I was amazed at how fast she could walk without tripping on her high heels. I had to run to keep up with her. When we arrived at the school, she skirted the long line of waiting mothers and their children and, holding my hand, went straight to the French policeman standing at the school's administration entrance. Distressed women yelled at us: "Who does she thinks she is? She should be in line like us."

The other policeman, an Arab, was yelling in Arabic at the noisy group of waiting mothers, and with a perceptible threat in his voice, he was shrieking at them: "Keep quiet! Keep quiet!"

Strolling and playing with his baton, he warned them: "Form a single line and keep quiet; otherwise you know what can happen to you."

Soulikah, ignoring the women's complaints, addressed the policeman in French, which I did not understand. Using her feminine charms, she introduced herself and they shook hands. Pointing her right index finger at me, she said to him something in French. She did not have to exhibit her identification, nor did I have to lie and declare my mother dead. When their polite male-female exchanges ended, they smiled at each other and she and I proceeded to the administration office for registration. The clerk registered me, and a few minutes later we headed back home armed with my school registration slip. Satisfied, Soulikah turned to me and said: "Shalom, how are you going to thank me for all this?"

I responded: "I always love you, and when I grow up I will buy you a present."

With tears in her eyes and joy in my heart, we hugged and kissed.

September 1930, at six and a half years old, I began attending Narcisse Leven school of the Alliance Israelite Universelle. (Seventy years later, in an article about Sephardic Jews, I learned about this great philanthropist who donated a great deal of money to build the school I attended. His charitable act helped revolutionize the thinking process of the new generation of Moroccan Jews and enriched our knowledge of the world outside the *mellah*. We leaped from the superstitious medieval realm into the twentieth century, a 500-year jump. The school was free, and the teachers were employees of the French government.)

The midday hot meal for all students was financed with donations of local wealthy Jews. The poor students, almost all, benefited from the meal, served in a huge eating hall equipped with benches and long wooden tables. Older boys directed younger ones to a sitting place and served the food. The meals consisted of an assortment of beans (to this day I shun beans) and a big chunk of dark bread. As soon as the blessing was said by one of the boys, we gulped the meal voraciously. Most times the meal was the important one of the day for many of us.

The Alliance headed two identical schools for the whole Jewish population of Casablanca. French and European students went to different primary and high schools. Their

Shalom Weizmann 21

schedule was different from ours. They rested on Thursday and Sunday, and the Alliance's schools closed on Saturday and Sunday. Children of wealthy notable Arabs had one school where Arabic and some French were taught. My school was divided in two equal parts, one for boys, the other for girls, with a capacity of 2,500 students each. In accordance with the French educational system, boys were physically separated from girls, and a concrete wall kept us apart. The girls' teachers were all women, whereas the boys' were men and women, Jews and Gentiles, all with diplomas from France. The classrooms were built on elevated concrete ground, and a large court denuded of trees separated section A from B.

Today my old school, under a different name, serves Arab students. It is located in the middle of Boulevard Moulay Youssef, where palm treetops sway to the breeze of the Atlantic. A block away are the U.S. and British embassies and the famous Boulevard d'Anfa leading to Hotel Anfa, where the Allied leaders met after the landing of the U.S. troops in North Africa at the end of 1942.

The school had nine grades, beginning with the highest number and ending with first grade. A diploma was given to students who passed the final exams. The latter were identical to the French exams in the mainland.

Because the Alliance schools were newly established in Casablanca, older boys and young ones began school at the same time, and a six- or seven-year-old boy might find himself sitting close to one who was eleven or thirteen years old. This created a terrible imbalance of physical power. Street-smart older boys took advantage of naive younger ones, and muscles dominated any argument.

My cousin Ayoush, a fifteen-year-old, was one of those older boys who began school at the age of ten. He was tall, strong and aggressive. My mother and I paid him a visit at the home of my aunt Isaa, who loved me a lot.

When Ayoush showed up, my mother addressed him: "Ayoush! I want you to consider my son as your younger brother. Please keep an eye on him and do not let anybody harm him."

On several occasions I used his name to intimidate those who harassed me. Ironically Ayoush abused me more than once. He had a tendency to mistreat others.

At the beginning of my school days, my father accompanied me to school, and after a while, at my insistence, he let me walk on my own to and from. I stopped going to the Heder except during the holidays when I accompanied my father. After school, I mingled with my friends, and as the spring came and the days grew longer, we lingered on our way back home from school. My being late created a lot of anxiety within my family, and my father was dispatched to look for me. He was so happy to find me that he forgot to scold me.

Time for the annual test of my first year in school had come, and the whole class was examined for our ability to read. A stout middle-aged woman came to my class and tested everyone. She sat on a chair facing the student and held a book on her lap. When my turn came, she asked me a math question and made me read a small paragraph in a French book. When I finished, she turned to my teacher and they whispered to each other. I did not understand what they said to each other, but I noticed their heads moving up and down in sign of acquiescence. The last day of school, my teacher, an attractive young woman told each student to what grade he should present himself in the subsequent school year. Because my name begins with a "W," I was the last to be told: "Shalom, you will go to grade 6. You skip grades 8 and 7."

I came home and reported the news to my mother: "Mamma, I am skipping two grades. The teacher told me that next year I will be in grade 6."

She silenced me by shutting my mouth up with her right palm. She pulled me close to her and said to me: "Do not tell any stranger about this." She feared for my life because of the evil eye.

My second school year found me in the 6th grade with Mme Termine. She was a skinny old woman who wore

Shalom Weizmann   23

thick glasses. We nicknamed her Aisha Kindressa, the witch
in the legends *A Thousand and One Nights*. She talked with the
distinct accent of the South of France and insisted we
memorize the weekly part of the Jewish Holy Bible in
French.

Next to me sat an older boy of eleven or twelve. At the
beginning he tried to harass me, but I stood my ground and
defended myself. When he tried to bully me, I threatened
him with my aggresive and combative cousin Ayoush. That
did the job, and after that I gained tranquility. I grasped the
study material pretty fast and tutored others who had a hard
time assimilating the subjects. I became respected among
my colleagues. We all lived several different lives in our
daily existence, speaking French in school, Moroccan at
home, local dialect with Arabs, and Hebrew in the
synagogue.

Each class organized a soccer team outside school. I
joined my class's team, and after school we gathered in
deserted fields adjacent to the school building and played
against other teams. For a ball we used a discarded silk
stocking. We stuffed the toe of the stocking with old rags
and tried to keep it round and firm as much as possible.
Then we tied the top and flipped the open flaps in the
other direction until we reached the end of the stocking. A
mother sewed the remaining open folds. It was a pretty
good ball, half the size of a legal soccer ball.

The next year I moved to grade 5, and two months later
I moved up to grade 4. (The school policy was to free as
many seats as possible to accommodate some of the waiting
children wishing to join the students' ranks.) Here older
boys talked freely about girls and sex. Some of them
smoked cigarettes in hiding and boasted about being able to
masturbate and attain a successful climax. I was catapulted
to a grown-up world where muscles were an advantage and
brains were useless outside the class. Boys waited for their
girlfriends coming out of the school next door.

In grade 4, my teacher was a Cary Grant type by the
name of Behar. Born in Istanbul, Turkey, he lived and

studied in France. Women teachers buzzed around him during the break. We gossiped a lot about his success with the opposite sex and envied him. He was a heavy smoker and could not resist lighting a cigarette during the class session, even though it was forbidden. He used to position me at the door so that I could alert him if someone was coming while he was appeasing his nicotine addiction.

To supplement his salary he gave supplemental studies after school hours to students who could afford the fee. They were very few, and even though he knew I could not afford a cent, he asked me to stay after class hours. We usually did our homework during those hours, and I always teamed up with a slow student and helped him.

Once a student named Albert challenged Mr. Behar's authority and refused to follow his dictate. The teacher said to the recalcitrant student: "Read the paragraph assigned to you and stop disturbing the class. Otherwise I will send you home with a bad note to your father."

Albert, a tall and muscular teenager, sliced the silence with his angry Arabic curses followed by words in French: "You do not scare me, Monsieur. I'm not afraid of you."

A heavy stillness ensued, and we all waited to see what was going to happen. In a slow motion the teacher took off his jacket and hung it on the back of his chair. He then rolled up his long shirt sleeves and, pointing at Kadosh, another strong tall student, he said to him: "You will be the referee between Albert and me."

Kadosh asked the teacher: "What should I do?"

Mr. Behar smiled and said: "I'm going to give Albert a lesson. We will have a boxing match in front of the class, and when one falls to the floor, you count to 10 and it is over."

He turned to me, and indicating the door, he told me: "Watch the door and alert me if somebody is coming."

I positioned myself so that I would not miss the combat while I watched the outside. Mr. Behar faced Albert and with an inviting gesture told him bluntly: "Come here, my friend, and defend yourself, big mouth!"

Shalom Weizmann 25

Albert stood erect, stretched his muscles and moved in a slow motion to an attack position. The teacher told him: "Defend yourself."

Before Albert realized what was happening, the teacher socked him twice with a left punch followed by a heavy right one. Albert fell to the floor. A trace of blood was coming out from the right corner of his mouth. At that moment I noticed a man coming directly toward our class. I closed the door and screamed: "Mr Behar! A man is walking in the direction of our class."

Hastily, Kadosh helped Albert get up. The latter cleaned up his bloody mouth with the back of his shirt sleeve and returned to his seat. The affair was closed. From that moment on, everyone in class knew his position in the hierarchy of things. After class we surrounded Albert and I dared ask him: "What happened to you, Albert. You did not even lift an arm to defend yourself?"

"Are you kidding!" said he. "My father would have massacred me if I was thrown out of school."
(In September 1944 after the Yom-Kippur fast, I met Mr. Behar at the home of a Jewish family in Marseilles, France. We both were serving in the French army during WWII. I reminded him of the year I was in his class, and he remembered me. We reminisced about a few things, among them Albert's episode.)

The fourth grade was a turning point for me. My body was becoming stronger, and I was welcomed into the dominant group of my class. I was nicknamed *Fil de fer* ("steel wire") because I was skinny and tall for my age. Boys spoke French in class, but as soon as we stepped out we resumed our Judeo-Arabic dialect. The girls spoke French in and out of class, and boys considered it very snobbish.

The subsequent year I spent in third grade with Mme Tabac, a sweet middle-aged woman from Paris. She put emphasis on correct French pronunciation. We learned a lot of French poetry and didactics. Half an hour's walk from our school there was a French school located in the Spanish neighborhood, contiguous to an all-Arab quarter. The school was exclusively attended by students of Spanish nationality. The French resisted mixing with Spanish or Italians, whom they considered inferiors.

In the middle of that school year, at the end of a school day, Spanish and Arab boys, an odd mixture, came in large organized groups and attacked us without provocation. They insulted us and threw rocks at us. Some of us were hurt, and our boys, unprepared, did the best they could. Strong boys took part in the battle despite the strict order of the principal, who forbade us to fight back. The skirmish lasted about half an hour before the police showed up. After this episode, with the intervention of wealthy Jews who bribed the French chief of police, the Alliance schools had two policemen, one French the other Arab, posted from morning to the end of classes on school days.

In that encounter, because I placed myself in the first line of defense close to my cousin Ayoush, I was hit by a sharp projectile that scratched my scalp. The wound was light, but I bled a lot and was taken to the school's first aid area to be cleaned and bandaged. Upon my return home the sight of my bloodied shirt and a bandage on my head unleashed from my mother a flood of tears, screams and curses in Arabic against my attackers. She asked me: "Who did this to you?"

I answered: "Spanish and Arab kids. I also threw rocks at them."

She resumed her cursing, this time in pure Castilian Spanish she had learned from her Spanish neighbor.

In the middle of that school year, Mme Tabac was replaced by Mr. Kaddosh. A calm and confident man, he was a father figure to all of us. Nobody raised his voice or argued with him. He was born in Algiers and also spoke Arabic, in a little different dialect from ours. I shared the school bench with my friend Jacob, who was my age and a sharp student. Jacob, who lost his father earlier, missed class two Thursdays in a row. The following day the teacher called him to ask: "Jacob, how come you missed two Thursdays?"

Jacob explained: "Mr. Kadosh. I'm an orphan and I need to help my mother support my brothers and sisters. I sell lottery tickets, and Thursdays are the best days for the sale, for Thursday night is when they play the national lottery."

Mr. Kaddosh was touched, and after giving the class a lecture about family relations, he described Jacob as a hero. He allowed him to skip class on Thursdays and assigned me to report to him the subjects taught in class that day.

My last year in school I spent with Mlle Sidi, a childless woman in her sixties who was a no-nonsense teacher. The first day of school, she introduced herself: "My name is Mademoiselle Sidi. Not Madame. You are here to learn and study. I will not tolerate any deviation from my program, and I hate perfume."

She humiliated students who did not bend to her wishes and spared no one. She especially disliked the few rich boys and verbally attacked them at every opportunity. During the course of the school year we all suffered her wrath one way or another. (See "Le Pauvre" story).

Jacob and I were the leading students in a class of forty-two. Through the entire year, Jacob was the head of the class except when I dethroned him the last month before the big tests. Finally, the final exams we prepared for had arrived. Two days of written and oral examinations, including some sports tests, took place in a different school. The whole class passed. Some got high marks; others just passed. I was one of those who just passed. In a small ceremony, the teachers and the principal handed us a diploma for public school completion.

We were relieved to get out of there. I was eager to shake away the burden of learning and studying. I was more interested in growing up, acquiring a trade, and earning wages. High school was out of the question. Poor people like me could not afford it. I was ten and a half years old when I hit the real world.

હ

Rama Weizmann

Normal

"Hey Ruthie, hurry up and finish making that chastity belt and let's go celebrate your birthday," my girlfriend Leona calls out as she walks into the shop where I work. It's a small store on Fourth Street in the heart of Greenwich Village where I handcraft leather bags and belts. Leona continues, "Hurray, you're finally eighteen and can join me in a legal drink on this gorgeous June day."

"I have to wait for Arthur Browne to return from dinner to take over the store. He's due about five." I continue struggling to squeeze a large metal spiral buckle through the loops of a wide leather belt.

Leona is dressed in a straight-lined black skirt which shows off the curves of her hips as she walks toward me in a swaying motion. She is a tall blonde who looks like a cross between Eve Arden and Lana Turner. Her sleeveless V-neck print blouse reveals the cleavage as well as a bit of each side of her breasts. Whenever we are out together, I can hardly push away a feeling of envy when I notice that men can't stop looking at her. I also experience a twinge of anxiety about our friendship. I come from a traditional Jewish family which is very puritanical in its attitudes toward sex. Virginity until marriage, motherhood, a nice home with venetian blinds on the windows are the normal goals for girls. I scorn these values, yet a part of me yearns to conform. Still, I am drawn to Leona — to her brilliant imagination, her humor and iconoclasm — like a desert traveler to an oasis. Leona is from an atheist, communist background. Once she confessed to me that her mother used to make speeches on soapboxes during the

Depression.

Leona says, "Relax. Your slave labor is only creating the latest fashions for parasitic bourgeois ladies who want to look bohemian and artistic." She lifts her eyebrows and tilts her head upward to indicate snobbery. "Remember what Karl Marx said about parasites. You should get yourself a real working class job, waitressing, like the rest of us. Shorter hours, better pay." She puts her hand in her purse and takes out a pack of Chesterfield cigarettes.

"Come on, Leona, you know there's no smoking here." She puts the pack back. I continue, "Listen, at my last waitressing fiasco I dropped a tray full of drinks. I swore that would be my final waitress humiliation. I can't help it if I am a klutz and can't hold a plate straight. I'm really grateful to Arthur Browne for teaching me to make these bags and belts. He once told me he learned this trade in a V.A. hospital, right after World War II, where he was recovering from a nervous breakdown. He said that Occupational Therapy made for his rehabilitation."

Leona smiles. "Some rehabilitation! Arthur Browne is so repressed he wouldn't look up from cutting his leather belts even if a naked lady belly danced in front of him. What a waste. So good-looking too."

"Stop making me laugh," I say. "God's gonna punish me for not finishing my work on time and laughing too much."

She replies, "Don't worry, Ruthie. God is always laughing at the antics of his crazy human creations."

Arthur Browne arrives exactly at five, and I give him my usual summary of what happened during his absence and then remove my apron. I am wearing a long flare purple skirt and white peasant blouse, with the sleeves above my shoulders. Leona and I are quite a contrast. I am short, dark-haired, thin and small-breasted. We step out into a glorious, sunny June evening where the leaves shine golden green on the skinny-trunked Manhattan trees rising up every quarter block from the concrete sidewalks. I reach into my purse for a Chesterfield, light up and deeply inhale. Leona does the same.

Exhilarated, Leona recites, "'The force that through the green fuse drives the flower. . .' oops, can't remember the rest of it. Come on, I am taking you to Mama Mennini's, a great Italian restaurant."

This is the first time I've eaten Italian food. My parents run a strictly kosher household. Leona orders lasagne for both of us.

"This is fantastic!" I tell her as I fill my mouth with the noodles, meat and cheese. "Definitely not kosher. God's gonna punish me for avoiding Friday night's boiled chicken."

"That's what I mean about you," Leona laughs in feigned exasperation. "You can't immerse yourself in the pleasures of the moment without feeling sinful. Here we are experiencing the superb oral delights of Italian cuisine, and you let a boiled chicken enter your head."

"Damn it, you're right," I reply. "Why can't I be a normal person?" We continue talking throughout dinner. When we finish eating, we immediately light up our cigarettes.

"I'll tell you what," Leona replies, "how about for tonight we give up our heroines Rosa Luxemburg, Virginia Woolf and Isadora Duncan, and pretend we are more like the girls in the Andy Hardy movies. Shit, I forgot the lead girl's name, the one who plays with Mickey Rooney. I think it's Ann Rutherford."

"Ugh, nauseating," I reply. "At least let me be Cathy in *Wuthering Heights* , swept up by Laurence Olivier as Heathcliff, or Ingrid Bergman in love with Gregory Peck in *Spellbound*." We giggle and fall silent for a few seconds. I then say, "Boy, this is a far cry from our discussions with Max and Sol at the Brooklyn College cafeteria. I wonder if they ever wish they were more like the sports guys, the ones who take girls to the proms. You know what I mean."

Leona smirks. "I doubt it. When Max discusses 'Do the ends justify the means?' or 'Does Stalinism flow from Bolshevism?' it's with the same passion as Clark Gable kissing Vivian Leigh in *Gone with the Wind*."

Rama Weizmann 31

I feel a tremor of guilt remembering the time Max tried to kiss me. I was horrified when he stuck his tongue in my mouth and pushed him away. It felt disgusting. Right after, Max was so sweet and apologetic. "How come we don't feel sexually attracted to any of the guys at our college table? They are all brilliant, caring. Did any of them try to make it with you, Leona?"

"Of course. They all did. But I told each of them it would be incest. Like sleeping with a brother."

"That must have hurt their feelings. Maybe that's why they have such trouble getting girlfriends."

"We are probably desexualizing them," Leona said thoughtfully. "Still we always tell them how much we admire, love and respect them in all other ways, and that is the truth."

I don't share with Leona my feeling that we are also not kind to one another in many important respects. We play intellectual one-upmanship games with the same intensity that delinquents play chicken in drag races. We try to wither whoever opposes our ideas, regardless of our close friendship. Sentences usually begin with sarcasm: "Didn't you know that?...How can you be so stupid?" We think we are sharpening each other's intellect by using this adversarial method. Our discussions invoke the same feelings I have when taking final exams. Despite the arrogant surface, I know we each have deep down fears locked in our own private torture chambers where demons sit and bludgeon us.

Leona interrupts my thoughts. "Hey, this conversation is getting too deep. Tonight is for you to have fun and celebrate. Let's get out of here. I am taking you for your first real alcoholic beverage in a bar."

We cut across Washington Square park where people are sitting around at the circle, a large metal rim bordering a fountain in the center that no longer works. Leona practically drools like an average teenager might about Frank Sinatra as she points to two guys sitting together on the circle: "That's James Baldwin sitting next to Anatole

Broyard. You know they are really good writers." I had not heard of either of them, but nod. We stop, and each of us lights up a cigarette and inhales deeply.

"Look at that Anatole. Gorgeous, slim hips. But they say he's gay."

I retort, "Oh you say that about every good-looking guy."

We walk another few blocks away from the Village toward Broadway. Leona stops at a brick building with neon lights flashing "Johnny's Bar and Grill." We enter a dark barroom with a sawdust-covered floor and sit down at a small table in the middle of the room. Leona tells me that this is a real bar for normal people. Not like the ones in the Village for gays, artists and intellectuals. Most of the people in the bar look like older men. A dyed-blonde drunk lady, who I immediately assume is a prostitute, sits on a bar stool leaning toward the man standing next to her. She is fingering his shirt collar as if to invite him to kiss her.

Fear, guilt and excitement boil inside me like a pot of soup cooking on the stove. I ask Leona what to order, and she suggests a Tom Collins for each of us. Our drinks arrive in a tall glass with fizzy water and a cherry at the bottom. After I take my first long sip, my head and arms feel airy. Guilt and fear vanish. Delight and excitement remain. We both light up.

Two tall, blond guys walk through the door, stand at the bar and order beer.

"Here they come, the normal Americans," whispers Leona. I stare up for a second at these two handsome fellows and then avert my eyes. We continue to talk about our friends.

A few minutes after our discussion Leona says, "Hey, I got an idea. Maybe we can get them to take us to the Friday night dance at the Hotel Atlantic."

"Wow, isn't that the place where your sister Janice's dates take her for dancing? I've even heard my cousin Anita say what a terrific spot it is for dancing. She once told me that during the war her mother went to USO dances there.

You know, to keep up morale for our boys."

"That's *the* place, the all-American dance floor. Remember Martin Block and Make Believe Ballroom time on the radio?" Leona replies. She then looks toward the two good-looking guys, smiles boldly and catches their attention. Her blue eyes balloon, a gesture she uses when flirting. They walk toward our table, stop and ask if they can join us. Leona points to the chairs and lets them know our names, "Leona, Ruthie." My cheeks are burning with embarrassment. They sit down, introduce themselves as Tom and Bill and order more beer.

During the conversation we learn they graduated from Madison High School a year ago and now work in a nearby warehouse. Both are waiting to be drafted for the war in Korea. I ask, "How do you feel about the war?" Each says he can't wait to go and fight the goddamned commies. Leona senses that I am about to argue that the war may not be justified, and she gives me a kick under the table to shut me up.

Luckily, Tom changes the subject. "We usually come here on Friday nights after work and dinner. The warehouse is nearby, in the Village. Boy, that Greewich Village is full of weirdos."

For a split second Leona clamps her lips together, signaling me to shut up. She then lifts her eyebrows slightly and stares at me with an expression I take to mean "You wanted normal manhood, well here it is." I have mixed feelings. Part of me wants to take on the guys about weirdos, but I restrain myself.

During most of the conversation Tom and Bill reminisce about the former joys of Madison High — where they played football and went to the dances — and brag how they just about got passing grades. We discover they are good friends and grew up together in Sheepshead Bay, Brooklyn, adjacent to Brighton Beach, where we grew up. To their, "Oh, Brighton, you must be Jewish," we counter with humorous defensiveness: "Oh, Sheepshead Bay, you must be Irish Catholic. Wanna make anything of it?" We

34   *Beneath the Rain Shadow*

tease and they laugh. They seem unprejudiced. Still, one never knows.

I ask, "What kind of work do you guys want to do in the future?"

Tom replies, "Maybe car mechanic, but first comes the army." Bill pipes up, "Hey, enough talk. How about us all going to the Friday night dance at the Hotel Atlantic?" Leona and I are jubilant, but say, "Yes, that would be nice," in restrained, lady-like fashion. We leave the bar, and they walk us to their shiny yellow 1949 four-door Mercury sedan, only a year old! I know car names and styles from a childhood street game in which the winner guesses the most names and styles of automobiles. But no one we know owns a car. We express our joy with "fabulous, incredible."

Bill drives, and Leona sits in front with him. After a brief discussion with many superlatives about the car, gaps of silence fill the fifteen-minute ride to Atlantic Avenue. Leona pumps for conversation by asking if they have a favorite movie and popular song. Their answers are brief: "Can't think of any just now."

Tom puts his hand on my elbow as he leads me into the ballroom. I am touched by the gentlemanly gesture, just like out of a movie. The ballroom is enormous and not too crowded, with enough room for each couple to move without bumping into anyone. The place is dim and has a pink glow to it. The big band is playing a Benny Goodman type rendition of "Sing, Sing, Sing." Luckily, Leona's sister taught us both to dance, so I know the basics. After initially feeling like a stick stuck in dough, I begin to loosen up. Tom and I start Lindying slow, with the basic steps of one, one two, back, one, one two, back. He then throws me out, and I boogie back, shaking my hips and shoulders. He twirls me around, and I don't even care when my skirt flies up with each twirl and reveals my underpants. I love to dance and am losing my inhibitions.

After a few Lindies, there are Rhumbas, and then Fox Trots. With each Fox Trot, Tom holds me closer. I feel uncomfortable but don't know how to squirm out of his embrace. I look over at Leona and she seems comfortable locked together with Bill. She's even leaning her chin on his shoulder, so I try to swallow my anxiety. During the last dance I feel something hard pressing against me from Tom's pants. I am afraid to think what it is. I can't wait for the dancing to stop and am so relieved when it is all over.

At midnight we return to the car, expecting to be driven home. I am in the back again with Tom. They drive to a deserted spot near the ocean at Coney Island and park the car. I'm near panic, but just ask, "What's happening?"

Tom pulls me down on the back seat and puts his hands on my breasts. I scream, "Hey, I thought you were decent normal guys. Stop." I push back hard. "You are a disgusting pig. I don't even know you. Get the hell off me."

Leona is in a similar position in the front of the car, but she always carries a hat pin inside her blouse. She maneuvers to get it out and jabs Bill with it. He lets out a yowl and backs off. She jumps out of the car and opens the back door and sticks Tom with the pin. He lets go of me. Leona grabs my arm and we run for the subway. They drive past us and scream out of the car, "Cock-teasing bitches!"

On the ride home Leona says, "You see, those guys are normal. Normal is not a long discussion in the Brooklyn College cafeteria. It's action."

Mariellen Houston Tissot

The Appraisal

No longer cradled in sleep, Allison wakes, the sun filtering in through white lace curtains. A small numbing fear scratches at the back of her head. Her mind darts in zigzags, trying to find a safe place to land. All the defenses she held during the day have slipped down around her ankles. The soft warm way sleep held her now cracks open and leaves her breathless, undefended and afraid. The house is empty.

She gets out of bed and walks down the hall, through the dining room, remembering where she hung out with her kids, past the mute piano, only the sound of her bare feet padding across the worn wood floors. The kitchen assaults her with its beauty. Smells of rosemary and sage fill her nose. She has been gathering it from her garden, hanging it to dry in the breakfast nook. She's taken advantage of the southern exposure, and now the sun pours in, almost blinding her, reflecting off the white tile floor.

Everything is white: the cupboards, the tile counters, the walls — except for the deep indigo blue glass streak which runs around the edges of the floor and across the tile backsplash. Stark and lovely. Everything she puts against the walls throws out color toward her. Even in winter when the sun is dim and waning, even then this is the brightest room in the house.

The sun spills pools of golden on her feet, making the morning seem welcome. But at night every sound in the house is a wordless threat, as if someone knows the kids are gone and she's alone. She toys with the idea of buying a gun but thinks it might be used against her. Maybe an alarm system would help. Turning toward the kitchen table, she sees the headlines from last night's paper. "Spokane woman raped and beaten," with the article: "Real estate agent raped and left for dead while holding an open house."

How many times has she been terrified? Coming home alone late at night after showing houses, running from her car to the front porch, fumbling for her key, always afraid some faceless stranger will drag her kicking and screaming down into the park. It happened to her neighbor. She shivers with the house, empty and alone. How much longer can she keep this job?

She tried talking to her broker about it, but he just said, "Allison, you can't sell real estate if you're afraid. If you can't stand the heat, get out of the kitchen."

The beeper signals from her briefcase on the kitchen table, and she glances at the clock. So early, too early to be calling. She picks up the phone to retrieve the message.

"I'll get you Monday, bitch, Monday," in a hoarse gravelly whisper. My God, who was that? It's Monday today. She pushes number 4 on the phone to get it to repeat: "Monday, bitch, Monday." She can barely hear it. She pushes 4 over and over again, trying to identify the voice. She can't make it out. It's too whispery, like fog rolling in on blue tendrils, each tendril squeezing her chest, cutting off air.

She clutches the edge of the table. The zigzag thinking starts again. Some weirdo out to bring her to her knees, to paralyze her with fear? Is it someone playing pranks, some kid randomly dialing numbers? What if it was the man from her open house? She has to go to his house tonight at seven to give him an appraisal. What if he's setting her up, only trying to get her alone? She can't just quit her job — three kids in college, a mortgage.

A dull metallic taste stings the back of her throat. She's had calls like this before. What woman hasn't? But she's getting older, almost fifty. When will she cross over the line and truly become an old woman? Not the body that still beckons, not the body to be violated. She carries her body like a shield, warding off the faceless strangers she fears, and God she doesn't want to go to the man's house tonight but she will.

Throughout the day she stays busy. Paperwork, telephone calls, always the threat of tonight looming: finally six o'clock forces her into her car.

Pulling up in front of his house, she sees why he liked her open house. It looks just like his, except it doesn't have a view. She smiles. She's sure he's not the guy who paged her this morning. He couldn't be. She's done appraisals hundreds of times. No big deal. The neighborhood looks nice; lots of people around. The evening is warm, a slight breeze ruffling the trees. Thank God it's still light out. She's wearing her real estate uniform — high heels, a suit, bleached blonde hair perfectly combed, red lips. A dusting of perfume on the inside of her wrist, the warm part, where blood runs through the blue veins, pumping and throbbing small waves of scent, rich and heavy, up to her nose.

She sees someone standing behind a fruit tree in the front yard, only his feet sticking out. Is that him? Why isn't he coming out to greet her? She gets out of the car and leans into it, riffling through some papers trying to get her nerve up to go in. There are people all around, up the street and standing in their yards. She turns toward the house. She can't let this fear get the best of her.

"Hello, Ted," she says as she goes up the stairs into the front yard. The house is set back on a huge yard. Nicely landscaped. At least he is taking care of it. He steps out from behind the tree.

"Hi," he said. "Allison, isn't it? I was just trying to figure out how to prune this tree. Come on in. I'll show you around. Can you give me a ballpark figure tonight? I mean, if this isn't worth enough, I won't be able to buy the other house."

"No, sorry, I can't. I've got to go back to the office and run the comparables. I want to get it right. It doesn't take me long. I can have it ready tomorrow."

She doesn't want to go in. She wants to get a better feeling about him. He's short — squat really — with a square body, wide face. Blunt-looking. His hair is coarse and stick straight. He's wearing thick glasses, so strong his eyes look little and far away. He's dressed in casual clothes — khaki pants and a clean pressed shirt. Expensive clothes. But there's something heavy about him — his body, strong and short; his hands, callused and square.

"Let's walk around the house," she says. "I'd like to see the back yard. It's really beautiful and so large for the neighborhood. Is it a double lot?"

She's stalling for time. She wants to see if there's an escape route from the back yard and if the neighbors can hear her if she screams.

"Yeah, it is a double lot. That's the one thing I'll miss in the other house. I like coming out here after work."

"I can understand that. It's really private. But look at the view you get in the other house, and the price is right too. It will only continue to appreciate. View property is really the best investment you can make. Don't you agree?" Are those her words? Is that her talking? She sounds like a record. Her heart slams in her chest. Her hands are shaking. She's got to go in or run from here, jump in her car, and drive home. She can't keep selling real estate if she feels like this.

"Well, are you ready?"

"Yes. OK."

"Let's go around to the front. The back door is locked."

They walk around the house on the small footpath. Manicured shrubs line the way. Late-blooming cherry trees shed their blossoms, dropping small pink polka dots on the ground. Feeling doomed, she makes her way to the front. He opens the door.

"C'mon in."

She walks through the front door and looks around. The house is neat enough, things put away. The living room is huge. A grand piano sits in the corner. It seems like a regular house, not some creepy dungeon with racks and chains on the walls. She starts to set her briefcase on the table and notices his house isn't really clean, not underneath. Everything is grimy. He has tried to straighten it up for her, but dust is everywhere. The dining room table has a kind of greasy film on it.

"I live alone here, and I'm not home very much."

She can tell. It's like a stage set. A trickle of fear creeps up the back of her neck, spreading into her jaw.

"It's really a lovely room, and so big," she says, trying to sound normal. It's true. Structurally the house is lovely, well built. The craftsmanship is exquisite. All the original details are intact: glass doorknobs, coved ceilings. Just the kind of house young professionals like. She's trying to stay close to the front door.

"Here. I'll show you the master bedroom."

Reluctantly she follows him. Pictures of naked women line the walls. Not tasteful nudes, but more like the pictures in a mechanic's garage — huge breasts hanging out over the bed. Red lips smiling out. Shivering, she wonders if this is what he likes. She thinks of her own body. Her breasts are large, straining against her suit, red cherries at sunset. She imagines him lying naked on his bed holding these pictures, remembering smells and touch, texture of skin so soft and warm. Does he touch himself and dream the smells of women deep and sweet? Standing in her suit, stiff and awkward, small beads of sweat forming on the palms of her hands, she imagines his hands touching her breasts, pushing her down on the bed. He could take her so easily, come up behind her and put his hands around her throat. Monday, bitch, Monday.

"Yes, quite a big room. Are there other bedrooms on this floor?" Ignoring the pictures, she walks out of the room.

"Yeah. Two more at the other end of the house, but let me show you the kitchen."

The kitchen is yellow tile, inset with small squares of maroon, forming diagonal patterns on the floor and above the sink. The appliances look old but clean, a perfect room really. Just the kind that sells well. The red evening sun spills in through the window.

"Oh, this kitchen is lovely. These are the original tiles, aren't they?"

"Yes. My parents owned this house, but I haven't done much to it. Do you think I should paint the kitchen?"

"No. It's fine the way it is. It's just what people like."

Her feelings are up and down. Fear and no fear. Going over her in waves, ebbing in and out over her, like the ocean pulling and releasing, waves so powerful she's losing her ability to see things clearly. But the kitchen is soothing, vaguely familiar. He hasn't made a move toward her. It's going just as it should. The wave subsides.

"Let me show you the basement. It's really nice." The place she doesn't want to go. But what can she say? She's the professional here. She has to look at the whole house.

"I don't have to go down. I mean, I've seen plenty of basements. It's really the first floor I need to look at."

"No, really. It's beautiful. I've done some work on it. C'mon. I'll show it to you. I'm really proud of it."

"All right. You go ahead. I'll follow."

Oh, God. He smells her fear. Smells it in her pores, her bones; sees it in her face, which is now a melting mass of jelly, the plastered red-lipped smile crumbling and dissolving. Her high heels sink in the plush carpet.

"See? Look. Isn't it beautiful?"

And it is. Recessed lighting, lovely curtains, a fireplace, thick carpet.

"Now, come look at the bathroom. I just had it finished."

She walks down a long hall. Now he's behind her. She couldn't get out even if she tried. She'd have to push him down, scramble over him, take off her shoes and run.

She enters the bathroom, and it's a masterpiece. Marble tub, huge and sunken; separate shower and marble basin. Gorgeous forest green tile on the floor. Plants and towels in varying pastel shades. Opulent, lush. Aftershave lingers in the air, sticking to the inside of her nose, the back of her throat.

"I really don't want to leave this house, but I've always

wanted a view of the water. Here, let me show you the furnace."

She walks back down the hall. He goes to a small door at the base of the stairs.

"What kind of furnace is it?" she asks.

"It's an oil furnace, the original one. I think you should take a look at it. I'm trying to decide whether to put in a new one."

He opens the door. Blackness hits her in the face.

"I think the light's burned out. Excuse me. It's on a string, if I can just find it." He puts his hand on her back, gently pushing her aside.

"Look out. There are paint cans down here. Let me find the light." His breath is on her. She can feel it on the back of her neck. Short puffs of air. She smells him. Aftershave mixed with sweat.

"Oh, that's all right. I don't really have to see it. Yes, yes, it's great down here."

She's backing up the stairs, words tumbling out. She's back in the yellow kitchen, the sun almost down, darkness covering the back yard like velvet. He comes up the stairs, and she walks quickly into the living room.

"I think I have everything I need. I'll just go back to the office and get this ready. What time would be good for you tomorrow? We'll go over it, and if it looks good, we'll write an offer on the other house. How does that sound?" She can't believe she sounds so calm. Her heart is hammering inside her chest.

"Tomorrow at this time will be fine. I have to work late, but I'll come home at eight, meet you, then go back to the office," he says.

"Fine. I'll see you at eight tomorrow evening."

She's out the door and running to her car.

"Goodnight." She waves as she gets into her car. She locks her doors and drives away, aware of him in her rearview mirror silhouetted against the light. His body looming toward her. Her foot is shaking on the gas pedal. Just keep the car going straight. Just head the car toward home. She's driving as if by rote, not wanting to stop for anything. Suddenly her beeper goes off. Pulling over to the side of the street, she picks up her car phone and dials her beeper.

"I'll get you Tuesday, bitch, Tuesday."

The hoarse gravelly voice clutches her throat. She pushes number 4 on her phone, getting it to repeat. Over and over again.

And It's Magic

randpa, Grandpa, where's the bean, where's the bean!" we all cry. Barbara, my younger sister, holds onto my mother's leg and sucks a tiny curl that clings to her cheek. *Ring around the rosy, pocket full of posy,* and the woodstove beats heat out into the shimmering kitchen, pricking my earlobes, sending tiny heat shivers up my back and against my cheeks, which are cold from the early October morning.

"The bean, Grandpa!" Sara and Barbara and I cry. Maybe he'll hide it in the pantry between the flour and the sugar sacks, or the jars of pickled beets. The wooden floors in the pantry are worn down by small feet thumping and running up and down. The shelves are packed. It's a small room off the kitchen behind the giant roaring cookstove that bubbles and brims with all of Grandma's stuff — creamed new potatoes from her garden simmering in a rich white sauce, peas from the vines, barbeque pork slathered with tangy red sauce, big crusty yeast rolls popped into the oven chamber next to the big roaring fire. The big black iron cookstove that fills the kitchen with warmth, red fire sending out wavery heat lines, which hold us in the house daring us not to go outside to the windy wintery Whidbey Island weather.

Oh, the wind blows all the time, whipping across

Crockett Prairie, careening around the house, bending the evergreens over and over, trailing branches against the house, while Grandpa's turkeys wail and gobble and strut up and down in their windy pens. We are whole in the wind in the middle of the stillborn kitchen.

The wind licks the flames of the woodstove down through the draft, driving the flames to fury. Red ball licks against the iron chamber, leaving a perfect brown crust on the rolls, golden yeasty orbs. And Grandpa sits in the corner with his great big farm boots, his overalls, and his tall thin body. His hair is combed over to one side, greased down with his good-smelling Bryl Cream, his dark tan face chiseled and bumped, his broken nose like a big Z.

"Now, babies, you know you've got to find the bean after it disappears," he tells us. He holds it up with two fingers for all of us to examine. "Now look at this, girls." And he twirls it around, showing us every teeny little mark it has. It's a dried-up kidney bean, and he's scraped some of the skin off, leaving crinkly red, then white, in special patterns. "Now y'all look at it real close, memorize it, cuz the first one who commences to find it will get the maple sugar candy."

And this is why we come. This is it. My mouth waters thinking of that candy — crusty and sugary on the outside, a thin layer of sugary maple; then inside, the smooth maple cream that fills my mouth and the back of my throat with sweet running maple. "Grandpa, Grandpa, do it!" we yell. And it's magic, cuz he holds it between two fingers and takes his other hand, brings it up, cups the hand, then *poof!* he opens both hands and the bean is gone, disappeared.

"Where is it, Grandpa. Where?"

"You've got to find it," he says and leans back in the wooden chair. "Go," he says.

I run into the pantry and it's dark in there. No big light hanging down, only what comes from the dusty window down at the end. The shelves are chock full — sugar and flour and big cans of lard and evaporated milk for Grandpa's coffee, and big tins of peppermint candy and jars filled with pickles floating in brine with big sprigs of dill and cloves of garlic turned brown by the salty vinegar, and hardtack and fresh loaves of bread and jars of green beans and corn and tomatoes, and sacks of things down by the window with writing on the sacks — coarse ground cornmeal or white flour or steel cut oats.

"Don't get them too excited, Jim," says Grandma. She's standing over her stove dipping spoons into bubbling things, opening the big hot fire door, bending down, wiping her face and always her cheeks, flushed and full, her white angel hair shimmering around her big beautiful face, her blue eyes deep and watery, looking at me.

"Now, girls, settle down," she says.

But we're running around the kitchen and the pantry screaming for the bean. "I'll get it first!" I yell, and I run down to the end of the pantry by the big dusty window. I fly into the stacks of sacks, feel the wooden windowsill, climb up on the cornmeal sack, and put my hand on the upper part of the window ledge. "I've got it!" I cry, and the smells in there just rip through my nose, tangy and sweet.

"No fair!" yells my big sister, Sara. "You found it too fast. No fair, Mom. She always gets it first." My pretty little mother stands by the back door, which leads to the tinny-smelling washhouse.

"Now Grandpa Jim, don't get the girls all riled up." But she's smiling at me. Daddy and Mom and Grandma look at us standing before Grandpa. I've got the bean in my hand. My sister takes it from me.

"Look at the marks, honey. Is it the same one?" Grandpa asks. And we turn it over and over in our hands — first Sara, then me. The bean seems the same. The white part under the crinkly skin which is pulled away is the same.

"Yes!" we scream together, "It's the same!" And the magic casts its spell on us. He made it disappear into the pantry. Made it fly through the air without us seeing it and land on the window ledge at the back of the pantry.

We hold out our hands for the sweet maple candy.

And the wind whips across the water up Crockett

Prairie, bending the big evergreens around the house, holding us in. The crows sing their simple song circling the house, and the woodstove pumps heat into the room, covering us with love.

The Gloaming

I love dusk,
I crave twilight,
when day begins to dissolve and
shafts and shards and skins of light
pull through the deepening of color
taking shape,
black and blue and reddening hue.
Night comes then, like velvet,
in gradual tones.

Evergreen

When the moon shines down and silver rain sheets against
   my window,
fierce winds howling the evergreens,
the rain beating inside my head,
Then I remember the featherbed, laid limp across the
hollow of my cheek
in Grandma's house,
night winds raging the trees,
bending them down to the shed
where the rooster cocked his generous head
and *Help*, I cried, as Daddy lifted the scarlet ribbon of my
   mind,
uncovering everything,
everything.
And Father, how much you've changed,
your leathery skin like paper.
Now the wind moves miracles across my mind

of freedom and warmth,
and it's heaven to be in the arms of my husband, lying on
    our bed, the open air arms of nature pulling us in.
And when the silver rain slashes against our window,
bringing the evergreen madness of childhood,
I hold it here, in my heart,
quilting for sacrifice, for love,
dark and brooding,
mending the frozen heart.

Haight-Ashbury

Think black, feel orchids in the night.
She's getting stoned, floating down Haight Street on a sunny
    day.
Then the boy steps out of a doorway. His mind is white
from all the acid he has dropped.
Blank spaces.
His hands are long, sinewy, fine.
His clothes drape on him, no distinguishing color, just an
 extension of his skin, soft beige.
He melts toward her. Light shatters off him.
He takes her down long hallways, up rickety steps
to sun-burned rooms.
She lays with him.
Love takes a turn and denies them,
holds back the flame of redemption.
She swims briefly into the space he opens for her into
nothingness
and fights to keep from falling.
She knows he wants to love her.
To wrap his brute dullness around the edge of her prickly
    soul
so he can stay alive, out of the acid ring.
Poor white boy, taking a chance with her.
He's losing his grasp
and she's too slippery to hold.

Lost Souls

He's dead, she said.
Are you sitting down?
No, I'm in the kitchen, standing by the beige tile counter,
little squares held together with mortar,
the way a chimney holds brick on brick.
But these are laid flat across the top.

Light breaks through the divider that separates
the family room from the kitchen,
and cubes of color break up space.
Out of the corner of my eye I see the coffee machine,
black and silver,
and the iridescence of the moon
shines through the window,
making halos around the room,
bouncing off the shadows.

I catch my breath and hold for minutes, eternity.

He's flying over the house, his soul is free.
Lost souls, I think, *ringing my house*
clamoring to get in.
I can't swallow when I hold my breath,
uneven ridges inside my mouth, pink flesh.

She doesn't say who's dead.
I know who, but she called me *honey,* which she never does,
so right off I knew it would be bad.
Strange, I thought my brother would make this call.

The top of my head is lifting off.
Mom, are you okay? my daughter asks me.
Yes, I say, thinking, *I've been waiting for this call for years,*
but I wasn't ready. We had so much unfinished business.
Half of my breath holds me back.
I can't release air.

My chest has not moved except by a fraction of sound,
which breaks clear in
my ear,

The piercing fear of it all
Because all time has fled through cracks in the wall,
The beige tile stands clear.
I rest my cheek on its cool dry surface
While the moonlight wavers around me.

Goodbye Daddy.

Jan Simpson

Shipping Out

The morning Brian left, Pam would be up early. It wasn't that he needed her up; he slept on, oblivious. It was she who needed the time alone. She'd shower and change into a pastel shirt and slacks, blow her graying blond hair dry, and draw a little lipstick across her thin cracking lips. Then she'd sit at the kitchen table nursing a cup of coffee and watching the sun begin its morning rounds of the backyard.

When the shower hissed to life again upstairs, Pam would get up to start breakfast. Glancing up at the clock, she'd pick up the coffee pot. She'd reach into the cupboard to get his favorite mug, the one with the picture of the Beechcraft Staggerwing, and set it at his place at the table. Brian would be drying his hair and packing his sea bag. He'd have just two hours left, enough time to eat and see the kids off to school. She'd lay a platter of pancakes and bacon in the center of the table, adjusting the knives and forks of the four place settings.

She knew the routine. She and Brian would sit for five or ten minutes while he surveyed the newspaper headlines over coffee. They'd talk about the weather, about Todd's sniffly nose and the doctor's appointment Pam had made for him, about Sara's cello recital and whether they'd ever be able to enjoy hearing the Bach piece again, about the crab grass and what kind of herbicide it would take to eradicate it.

Then Todd would come down, carrying his Air Cruiser Batman, the latest in his collection, and rubbing the sleep from his eyes. His father would admire the well-armored superhero as Todd flew it around the kitchen, complete with sound effects, one more time before plopping down in his chair and dragging the plate of pancakes to himself. The two would talk soccer. Mouth stuffed with pancakes, the boy would recount all the great saves he'd made in the game last Saturday. Brian would smile and pat him on the back, announce that undoubtedly his son was going to grow up to be the best goalie in the history of the sport. Pam would remind Todd about his homework, ask if he'd done his spelling words, and the male contingent of the family would turn in unison to scowl at her for disturbing them with such trivialities.

Sara would drag herself to the table last, and only after Pam called up the stairs to remind her that she'd be late for the school bus if she didn't hurry, and after Brian followed that up five minutes later by hollering that if she didn't stop brushing those blond curls, they'd fall out from the wear and tear and she'd have to go to school bald.

So Sara would give it up and dribble herself down the stairs, stopping to check herself again in the mirror by the front door, grimace, and drop despondently into her chair at the kitchen table. Then she'd proclaim once again that life was hopeless for anyone who looked like she did. If only she had Marcia Torrance's thick black hair instead of the thin wispy strands her mother'd cursed her with, if only she had Carla Anato's dark seductive eyes instead of her father's pale greys... If only Sara could look in the mirror and see the person her parents saw instead of the hideous creature she fantasized herself, Pam thought. But then she wouldn't be twelve.

Meanwhile, none of them would mention the sea bag by the front door.

The leaving always began about a week before Brian took his next duty rotation. Three months out on the sub, three months home. And, of course, Pam could never ask where he'd be. That was classified.

It started with little things. Maybe Todd's school would

send home the announcement about Parent-Teacher night. And Brian would have to explain to the boy that Mom would have to meet Mrs. Gardiner this time, but she'd brief him when he got back home.

Or Mrs. Hanson would schedule a recital for Sara, and Brian would have to explain he wouldn't get to hear her play the Bach piece in front of all the parents, but maybe she could play it one more time just for him the night before he left.

Within a day or two, both kids knew the program. They brought everything to Mom directly, as if he'd already left.

Brian always spent more time at the base that last week, stayed out with his buddies a little later, drank more than he should. And Pam became more attentive to the housecleaning, the laundry, the kids' homework, her night class in Spanish.

They never made love — or even had sex — the night before Brian left, sometimes not for several nights before. As the day for shipping out approached, a wall grew, a few bricks at a time, down the middle of the bed. Pam felt herself withdraw behind it, steeling herself against the eventuality of the empty bed. If it bothered him, he never said so, as if he felt he deserved nothing better.

The morning he had to leave, Brian would sit there, sipping his coffee after the kids had boarded the bus. He'd review the finances for the eleventh time as if he thought she'd never handled a dime in her life, then reluctantly hand over his checkbook. He'd remind her to put oil in the car and tell her everything she should say to the repairman when he came to check the hot water heater. Then in the last fifteen minutes, he'd fall silent.

He'd stare intently out the window at the basketball hoop over the garage door, at the azaleas in the garden, at the rope swing hanging from the Quasimodo oak in the corner of the yard. He'd listen to her tell about the shouting match the Navy couple next door had the other day in their driveway in front of God and everyone, about her expectations that their house would be up for sale in a divorce soon. But he'd listen with half an ear. Pam knew he was collecting the sound of her voice more than what she was saying, mixing it with the shrill of the starlings who'd nested in the eaves of the garage; the low woof of Pups, their Labrador, in the backyard; the grind of the garbage truck making its way through the neighborhood — filing it all away inside like a time capsule he would savor later.

Then his buddy Marty would be by to pick him up. They'd hear his Dodge truck growling in the driveway. And Brian would get up, give her a quick peck on the cheek, grab his sea bag, and head out the door. And Pam would sit there with a cold cup of coffee, the warmth ebbing from the empty chair beside her and three long months in front of her.

The first couple of days were the worst. The kids would be horrible. Todd would get in a fight with some bigger kid at school and come home with a Rudolph nose. Pam would end up in a fight with her daughter over wearing makeup to school. Then the kids would be wonderful. Suddenly they'd clear the table and take care of the dishes without being asked, as if they were afraid their mother would disown them and they'd have no one. But that would pass, too. It always took a few days to get a routine, a rhythm everyone could live with. She'd know they'd found it when they all went back to being themselves, neither demon nor angel.

Subconsciously avoiding the bedroom at first, Pam would stay up late watching Murphy Brown and Mary Tyler Moore reruns, fall asleep finally on the couch in front of the TV. Within a week or so, as the sense of Brian faded into obscurity, she'd be sound asleep by ten, enjoying the luxury of the middle of the bed.

Likewise, the first week, the kids would be missing Dad, but they'd manage. Todd would start ticking off the days on the calendar until his dad's return. By the end of the second week, they'd forget to miss him. The boy would announce he was going to tick off each week instead. He'd remind her again that Dad promised to bring him a surprise. And after that, Dad would be just a pleasant memory, like a playful uncle who'd come to visit for the summers.

For ten weeks Pam would run the house, pay the bills, attend PTA meetings, volunteer at the Red Cross, drive kids to lessons and Scouts, listen to her Spanish tape in the car between errands, help with homework, mow the lawn, take the dog to the vet, play canasta with three other Navy wives one night a week, and work part-time three mornings a week at the Commissary. It wasn't that she didn't miss Brian. There were times. Whenever they played "Staying Alive" on the radio. Whenever she smelled his aftershave on some guy going by in the mall. Whenever she ended up behind some fellow over six feet tall with curly brown hair in the supermarket, until he turned around and didn't have those intent grey eyes and that smile that spread left across his face like slow honey.

And then one day they'd all remember. Todd would realize that he forgotten to tick off three calendar weeks and run in to the living room to announce Dad would be home in ten days.

Then they'd go through the leaving pattern in reverse. One morning Sara would make her bed and clean her room in anticipation of Dad coming home. The next day Pam would tell her it was too late to call Marcia, and they'd end up in a tear-filled row in which Sara'd be sure to tell her mother she was a first-class witch. Todd would line up his squadron of fighter planes across the door to his room for Dad to see, then melt down when they had to be picked up for the vacuuming. And Pam would lie awake after they'd both gone to sleep, wondering which she wanted more, having him home or having him away.

It had started after Sara was born and the newness of marriage was behind them, a gnawing dread that grew on her for the three months Brian was away, a dread of his first night home. He'd arrived on the doorstep with that overbearing grin on his face. He'd hugged Pam tight enough to crush and made some remark about how good it felt to have something warm and voluptuous against his chest. His eyes pursuing her, he'd waited impatiently until the kids were in bed or gone to school, then suggested they take a shower. Of course, every touch of his hand found its way somewhere suggestive. It wasn't that she didn't want to. Some part of her did. But the first feel of him wasn't the warm welcome of a long-lost lover. Her body went on red-alert at the touch of a seeming stranger.

She'd tried at first to suppress it. After all, he was her husband. Her body was just behaving badly. Guilt-ridden, Pam pressed it into service. She'd stand there in the shower, letting Brian satisfy three months of touch deprivation, hearing him hum deliciously to himself, whisper in her ear how much he'd missed her, how he was still married to the sexiest woman in the world.

She knew it was all meant as a compliment. But as he lay snoring beside her afterwards, Pam hated her body for its treason and she hated herself for not listening to it. She thought about telling Brian how she felt, that she needed more time to accept him back into her space, to hear his deep infectious laugh, to watch him play Dad, to remember the man she'd fallen in love with in the first place. She could imagine already the look on his face, a cross between hurt, hostility, and an indictment of insanity. Why should a man be expected to woo his wife again and again? He had enough on his plate to support them. Shouldn't he be able to expect that ground taken in conquest stayed taken while he was away?

So she'd taken to being aloof, having headaches, pretending some offense that needed mending. And in time he had backed off, giving her a wider berth on his arrival home. Then she hated herself for her dishonesty even though she loved the quiet way he sought to win her over again. Why did it have to be so difficult?

Her waning physical attachment to Brian in his absence as the weeks wore on was quietly disconcerting. But more mortifying were the fantasies that crept in to replace it. The sacker at the grocery store who smiled as he asked Pam if she needed help with her groceries, the head librarian who helped her find books for Sara and Todd, the vet who gave Pups his shots — they all began to look like romantic possibilities. By ten weeks out, even Jack — the short, stocky, balding shelf-stocker at the Commissary who whistled through a small slit in his front teeth while he worked — was looking pretty good.

Jack was an old-fashioned guy who could still remember the days before political correctness, when it wasn't a crime to admire a girl from a distance. He never missed a compliment when Pam had just had her hair done, knew when she had new clothes. She'd find herself hanging around the coffee room over lunch, chatting with him just to pass the time. The longer she talked to him, the more he got to looking like Yul Brunner.

Was it so much to ask? To be treated as if you were still worth the initial effort of the win? To have a man eye you approvingly from a distance before myopia took over? And just about the time Pam was contemplating that thought, she'd come to find she'd been standing in front of the mirror for nearly an hour, combing her hair aimlessly as she studied her face for wrinkles. To compensate for her mental transgressions, she'd take to brown-bagging her lunch to the park and avoid Jack for the rest of the tour of duty.

The end would come finally. She'd fall into an exhausted sleep about four in the morning, knowing Brian would be home in just six hours and she still had the kids to get off to school. Next morning after they'd gone, Pam would sit, stirring her coffee absently, hearing the tick of the kitchen clock behind her. Then she'd hear Marty's truck drone into the driveway and catch sight of the curly brown hair and broad shoulders as Brian unloaded his sea bag from the back. And he'd wave Marty off and lumber up the walk. He'd pause this time to eye the For Sale sign on the house next door and shake his head. He wouldn't spot the pansy border she'd have put up one side of the walk. Later he'd tell her he knew there was something different about it, he just didn't know what.

Then he'd see her sitting in the window, watching him.

He'd wink, and that slow smile would ripple across his face. And then like some modern-day Merlin, he'd pull a tissue-wrapped bundle of red roses from under his arm.

And she'd forget all about the sacker and the librarian and the vet, and even Jack, and recognize she was going to betray herself again. That was the problem with love.

Sandra McGillivray Ortgies

Lanterns
An Island Mystery

The beach house lights dimmed, held on a flicker, then in slow motion came up to brightness again. "Damn! Not tonight." Connie waited beside the bed, willing the morning glory shade on the antique lamp to keep shining. The winter wind off the Sound was getting stronger, whipping giant firs into bowing submission while a rogue log pounded the seawall until Connie anticipated the thud like a heartbeat.

Connie slipped a carnation into the pewter vase on the night stand before working her way back along the hall, dusting the ornate frames surrounding the "greats." The old photographs had been of interest, and some amusement, to their guests. Her great-grandmother Ellen was such a reasonable-looking woman that it was reassuring to Connie to take a glance at her in the course of a hectic day. Ellen was gazing steadily at her when the lights went out. The refrigerator stopped humming, and the lilting Joplin music abruptly quit, followed by a "what-are-you-going-to-do-about-it?" silence.

"I'll get the lanterns going in here," called Alex from the living room. "Are the flashlights already in the guest bedrooms, Con? We're in for it tonight."

At least they were prepared. Alex had started collecting lanterns and oil lamps when he'd found a conductor's lantern at an Island garage sale. Now, eighteen lanterns and oil lamps decorated the living room nooks and shelves. One time he'd lighted them all, and they'd reminded Connie of

Sandra McGillivray Ortgies 59

a diverse group of people coming together with a common purpose: hard-working barn lanterns, sturdy train lanterns, and graceful old oil lamps glowing in elegance.

Alex turned from lighting the fire as Connie followed her flashlight beam into the room. "Well, we promise the guests a romantic stay," he shrugged, "so that's what they're going to get." She came up behind him and ran her hand along the strong line of his back as he hunkered down in front of the fireplace, feeding more kindling onto the grate.

"We'll have to keep them in here with us by the fire this evening. It'll get cold fast in those back rooms," said Connie, pulling a rainbow stack of afghans from a window seat and setting them along the backs of chairs. "Since they're coming for the Mystery Weekend, maybe they'll think a power outage just adds to the occasion."

A set of headlights swept into the driveway. *Masseys or Fortins?* wondered Connie. She grabbed their elkhound Talley by the collar and scooped up Nacho, the chunky orange-striped cat. "You might be introduced later," she told them, unhooking Nacho's claws from her sweater as she settled them in the third bedroom before going to the door.

"Welcome to Lanterns," said Connie, keeping a firm grip on the massive wooden door as a gust of wind pushed against it. "Come in and get warm by the fire."

"Sounds good," said the tall, graying man carrying a hang-up bag. "I'm Brad Massey. This is my wife, Jenna."

"Oh, this is lovely," said Jenna, shaking Connie's hand. "We've been wanting to get away for a holiday, and the Mystery Weekend was all the excuse we needed." She paused at the living room entryway as her husband hung the bag on the hall tree. "Lanterns and oil lamps all around. What an inspired touch!"

"The plus side of a power outage, but it could come back on any minute," said Connie, trying to convince herself. "I'd like you to meet my husband, Alex. We have two more guests arriving soon; then we'll have coffee by the fireplace." Brad Massey shook hands with Alex, then eased his lanky frame into the maple rocking chair as Jenna smiled at Alex and turned to warm her hands at the fireplace.

A loud pounding at the door turned their attention to the entryway. *Must be the Fortins,* thought Connie as she excused herself and went to the front hall. As Connie swung open the door, she thought she'd never greeted two more subdued, grim-looking guests. "We've been expecting you. Please come in." Connie stepped aside, knowing the warmth of the lantern light behind her was as beckoning as the candlelit windows in a Kinkade painting. It seemed lost on these two, though.

"You must be Connie Ross. We spoke on the phone last week," snapped Ron Fortin, propelling his wife into the living room. "I still have no idea what we're doing over here this time of year. Some notion of Fiona's. Mystery Weekend! The mystery is why I let myself be talked into it."

What a charmer, thought Connie. *Thank goodness for the Masseys.* Alex made introductions all around, as the Fortins settled themselves at opposite ends of the sofa.

"Tell me, is this part of the 'mystery ambiance,' or are you just saving on electricity here?" asked Ron Fortin, tossing both needlepoint pillows from the sofa to the floor beside him.

"I think it's delightful," said Jenna, her British accent politely putting Fortin in his place. "We're far too dependent on modern conveniences. I, for one, hope the power stays out all weekend."

"You're an incurable romantic," said her husband, smiling.

"Absolutely, darling."

Fiona Fortin had yet to say one word. The easy banter between the Masseys seemed to cause her to shrink back into the sofa cushions, staring at the crackling flames. Alex might say Connie was reverting to her psychotherapist role, but anyone could see Fiona Fortin was in emotional distress.

Alex offered brandy with the coffee Connie had made in an old percolator on the camp stove. They didn't usually offer liquor to guests, but she agreed that it seemed like a good idea tonight to counter more than one kind of chill. Brad Massey was attempting to draw out Ron Fortin about his computer business in Seattle, and while Connie sat listening to Alex answer Jenna's questions about the Island, Fiona walked stiffly to the sideboard and helped herself to another shot of brandy.

It's going to be all right, thought Connie, resting her head against the smooth fabric of the wingback chair. They were warm and, with the exception of Fiona, relaxed. The wind set a pine bough to rhythmically scraping against the house like the brushing beat of a jazz drummer, and Connie was getting drowsy.

A rapid tapping at the sliding glass door startled them all. A tall shadowy figure was on the patio off the living room. *I don't like this,* she thought, but there was only one person, at least right at the door. Alex slid the door back. "Come in. How can we help you?" An icy draft whirled the length of the room, causing the flames to flare up in the grate before Alex could get the door pulled shut again.

"Sorry to bother you," said the man, standing awkwardly inside now, smoothing back his rain-soaked hair. "I need to use your phone. My truck died at the corner; looks like I'll have to get a tow truck out here. Alex checked the directory, dialed, and handed the phone to him.

Connie was passing a tray of pastries to Jenna and Brad when Fiona swung right around on the sofa. *What is her problem?* thought Connie. *Now she's staring at this guy.* He glanced around the group, then turned his back on them to speak lowly, finishing with, "OK, twenty minutes. I'm at the crossroads." He hung up and turned to Alex. "Thanks. I'll wait in the truck." He slid back the door and went out into the slashing rain, his poncho billowing behind him.

"We'd never let anyone into our house like that in the city," said Ron. "You never know who's packing these days."

Connie had to admit she'd had momentary qualms about letting a stranger into the house. As obnoxious as Ron Fortin was, in this instance he might have a point. Alex chose the moment to stretch and yawn, with the desired result.

"I don't know about the rest of you," said Brad, "but I'm ready to turn in. Coming, Jenna?"

"Yes, we've got to be sharp for those mystery clues," she said, gathering her leather bag. "Goodnight, all. See you at breakfast."

Connie picked up her flashlight and led the way to their room. She was regretting she'd given the Masseys the back bedroom overlooking the garden. It was attractive enough, with French doors opening out onto the private patio; but she'd rather they had the knockout beachfront suite.

Ron was on his feet glaring at Fiona as Connie came back into the living room. "You go on to the room," he ordered, shrugging into his jacket. "I'll get the stuff from the car."

Fiona jerked her head up, startled from her trance-like staring into the fire. Connie crossed the room and gently touched her shoulder. "I'll show you to your room now, Fiona. You can walk right around from the parking area, Ron. Fewer steps."

Ron snatched the old log-boom lantern with its over-sized reservoir from the hall table and slammed the door behind him. *Could have been the wind,* thought Connie, but Alex looked up at her and shook his head as he banked the fire for the night.

"High winds frighten me," whispered Fiona. "Do you think the storm will be over soon?" She was holding Connie's hand as they made their way along the hall between the "greats." Connie could have sworn Great-grandfather William raised an eyebrow as she glanced his way in the lamplight.

"Oh, before morning, for sure," replied Connie. "These storms and power outages are a regular winter occurrence here. Our trees have withstood much higher winds than this. They're just noisy about it."

The oil lamp Connie carried gave the beachfront room a warm glow, and for the first time Fiona looked around with interest. Even with the fabric blinds lowered over the big windows, the sea was only thirty feet away, and Connie knew the measured crash of storm waves against the seawall, coupled with the wind-driven howl of the big trees, was going to set Fiona off again at any moment. "Your husband will be coming around to this door, Fiona." Connie walked over and turned back the deadbolt lock. "The parking area is just around the corner of the house at this end." She set the lamp on the table and turned back the comforter, not wanting to leave Fiona alone but hoping to be gone before Ron came in. It was time to be off-duty. She'd had enough of the Fortins for one evening.

Alex and Nacho were already in bed when Connie entered their room. "I definitely do not want you or Nacho to meet Ron Fortin," she told Talley, who was lying in his favorite spot beside the bed. "He'd warp you for sure. Alex, I'm worried about Fiona. Something's wrong, and I can't get a handle on it."

"Didn't we agree you wouldn't analyze the unsuspecting guests?" said Alex, glancing up from his book. "The Masseys couldn't be nicer, and sure we could do without the Fortins; but that's the way it goes. I wouldn't be surprised if they head back to the mainland tomorrow."

Morning dawned with that bright crispness that happens only after a storm. The sand was strewn with limbs and debris from the towering evergreens. White-capped waves danced a retreat on the outgoing tide, leaving a ribbon of bark slivers on the shoreline.

Best of all, thought Connie, the power was back on and the smell of coffee filled the breakfast room as Brad and Jenna hesitated in the doorway. "Good morning! Come in and join us," said Alex, reaching for the coffeepot on the sideboard. The small room, decorated in tones of terra cotta and adjacent to the kitchen, was a favorite retreat for Connie and Alex as well as their guests. Shallow bowls of blooming paper-white narcissus leaned into sunshine beaming across the hardwood floor through full-length windows.

Brad and Jenna were dressed in jeans and boots, with heavy wool sweaters over flannel shirts, ready for their day of hunting clues and suspects. *Sleuthing, Northwest style,* thought Connie with a smile, as the Masseys sat down at the round table. "We won't wait for the Fortins," said Connie, on her way to the cobalt-blue tiled kitchen. "Apparently they're sleeping in, and we know you're eager to begin your day in town." Alex filled their coffee cups as Connie returned with a tray containing juice, cereal, and her specialty: home-made scones with local loganberry jam.

It was after ten and there was still no sign of the Fortins when Alex came in from walking Talley out to the mailbox. "Connie, their car's gone. I think we'd better see what's going on."

The door to the beachfront room was locked, and repeated knocking brought no response. Alex called, "Hello, Ron? Fiona?" then took out his keys and unlocked the bedroom door. Nothing. No Fortins and no luggage. The bed had not been slept in.

"This is a first," said Alex.

"I'm glad they're gone, but wouldn't you think they'd at least let us know?" said Connie. She glanced around the room again. Something should be here that wasn't. "Alex, Ron had the boom lantern with him when he went out for the bags; it's not here."

"Even if they needed the lantern to walk out to their car in the dark, they could have left it beside the garage," said Alex. "It's one of the rare ones. I'll give them a call later and find out what happened."

Connie could tell that Alex was pondering the entire Fortin fiasco as he poured them each another cup of coffee. This disappearance was worrisome. Guests were usually pleased with their weekends at Lanterns and told them so.

They'd settled back with their favorite sections of the newspaper when Talley alerted them that someone was on the porch. Talley rarely barked, relying instead on a riveting stare. *Rather like Fiona,* thought Connie.

Alex opened the door. It was Jim Hobson, the sheriff.

"Morning, Alex, Connie. I need to talk to you," he said, getting right to the point of his visit. "Did a couple named Fortin call or check in here last night?"

"Yes, they came in about eight," Alex said, looking at Connie. "But they left sometime in the night. What's the problem, Jim?"

Sheriff Hobson glanced over his notes as they sat at the kitchen table. "There was an accident last night on the Harris Road where they've been clear-cutting that acreage. One of the firs in the buffer came down on the road, right on the Fortins' car. He died at the scene; she's at the hospital with multiple injuries, still unconscious." The sheriff wrapped both hands around the steaming mug of coffee Alex handed him. "I just came from the accident scene. The deputy found your brochure on the back seat."

Connie felt sick and fought a surge of remorse. Why did they take off in the storm? She and Alex had tried to make them feel secure and comfortable. Why would they leave the house? Fiona had been afraid of the storm. It must have been Ron who decided they'd leave.

Connie came out of her reverie to hear the sheriff ask Alex if he would come to the hospital to identify Ron Fortin. "I want to go too," she said. Perhaps Fiona would be awake; and even if she wasn't, Connie thought she could at least sit with her.

The police cruiser seemed to float along the island highway in the sparkling sunlight. Even with her lined raincoat belted tightly around her, Connie couldn't seem to get warm. Everything looked so normal, and Ron Fortin was dead. Yesterday at this time, he probably was still at work, harassing his employees, regretting that he'd agreed to Fiona's weekend plans.

At the hospital, Connie and Alex followed the sheriff to Fiona's room. Her small body seemed almost lifeless in the elevated bed. The other bed in the room was empty. Alex pulled the armchair close to Fiona's bedside for Connie. "I'll be back soon," he said, following the sheriff out of the room.

"Fiona, can you hear me? It's Connie Ross from the bed and breakfast. I'm so sorry."

Fiona's eyelids twitched. Her lips moved as she struggled to get words out. It was as if her mouth wouldn't shape to the sounds she was trying to make "Cuh, cuh," she rasped. She clutched at Connie's hand.

"Yes, Fiona, it's Connie. I'm right here." Fiona's eyes suddenly opened wide with a beseeching look that brought Connie close to tears. Then her eyes closed again and she slipped back into unconsciousness.

Connie was holding Fiona's hand when Alex and the sheriff came back into the room. "Alex, she woke up. Just for an instant, but she woke up."

"Step out here with me for a moment, Connie." Alex held the door open for her as the sheriff took her place in the chair beside Fiona's bed.

Alex leaned wearily against the wall. "That's not Ron Fortin down there in the morgue. It's the guy who came to the door last night to use the phone."

"What? Alex, are you sure? I mean, who is he? Why would he be driving the Fortins' car?"

"There's a lot we don't know. He didn't have any ID. The big question now is, where's Ron Fortin?"

***

As they turned into their lane, Connie was struck with how familiar and solid the house looked while she had this feeling of dangling in time. Had it been only two hours since they'd left to go to the hospital? The sheriff parked at the end of the parallel rows of bare apple trees. "Let's have a look at the room first," he said, starting up the sidewalk.

Alex unlocked the door of the beach house and automatically stepped aside as Talley barreled past them down the stairs to the backyard. Connie led the way along the hall to the beachfront room at the far end of the house. She raised the pleated blinds as Alex checked the closets and bathroom. "Where does this door lead?" asked the sheriff.

"Out to the deck and hot tub; then a path goes around

Sandra McGillivray Ortgies 67

the house to the parking area," said Connie. "Ron brought their bags in that way last night; at least that was where he was headed the last time we saw him."

They filed out onto the deck, Talley snuffling along beside them after chasing around from the far side of the house. The deck had been of great interest to the old dog ever since an otter had settled under it for a few weeks the previous fall. "Talley, stop that; come here," called Alex as the dog leaped to the ground and pushed his way under the deck. They all heard the faint groan coming from farther under the deck. Alex and the sheriff jumped down off the deck, pulled Talley back, and knelt on the ground cover.

Looking down at them, Connie could see glass shards glinting in the ivy, and off to the side in the wild grass was the bare metal frame of the log-boom lantern.

Alex crawled under the deck. "It's Ron Fortin and he's hurt," he shouted. "Let's get him out of here." Between them, they eased Fortin out onto the grass. Connie ran back into the bedroom to get blankets while the sheriff radioed dispatch for an ambulance.

Connie helped Alex cover Fortin with the blankets, then followed the grassy path beside the house, retracing the steps he would have taken bringing their bags in. In the soggy ground, she discovered one set of large footprints coming toward the house from the parking area and dual footprints leading away from the house. A pair of high heels and, in long strides, cowboy boots.

The sheriff and Alex were talking with the EMTs on the far driveway to the boat launch as they loaded the stretcher bearing Ron Fortin into the ambulance. Connie walked over to the sheriff and described the footprints as Alex coaxed Talley back inside and locked the door. Alex and Connie, in their Jeep, followed the ambulance and sheriff's car down the road to the highway. "Jim's going back to the accident scene on his way," said Alex, as the police car turned off on a side road. "We'll see him later at the hospital."

Alex and Connie ran into the ER to find Ron Fortin

awake on a gurney. The bandages on his head looked like a helmet above his swollen face. *Raisin eyes in a bread dough face,* Connie was thinking, when he whispered, "Fiona."

"She'll be all right, Ron. Can you tell us what happened?" asked Alex. "Did that guy who came in to use the phone last night do this to you?" Ron grimaced and closed his eyes.

The ER tech pushed the gurney along the hallway and into the room where Fiona, still unconscious, looked as pale as a porcelain doll. Ron leaned toward her as Alex helped the technician move him into the other bed. "Don't worry, Fiona. I'll take care of you."

Fortin looked up at Connie and Alex. "You two don't need to stay around. I'll take over now." Despite his battered appearance, Ron seemed alert and calm after seeing Fiona. Connie realized they hadn't had anything but coffee all day, and she was hungry. Alex seemed to read her mind.

"Listen, Ron," said Alex. "The call button is on the pillow beside you ... if you or Fiona need anything. We'll get a bite downstairs and be back in a little while. The sheriff's going to want to talk to all of us as soon as he gets here."

At three in the afternoon, the cafeteria was almost deserted as Connie and Alex sat eating their sandwiches. Sheriff Hobson was waiting for the elevator when he saw them through the glass door and slid in beside Alex on the bench. "We found the victim's wallet wedged under the front seat. His name's Carl Addison. Does that name mean anything to you?"

"Carl Addison? ... No," said Connie. "He wasn't in the house more than ten minutes. He literally blew in, used the phone, and left."

"No one paid much attention to him," added Alex.

The scene jumped back into Connie's mind. "Wait a minute, Jim. Remember, Alex? Fiona did. She'd been acting like a zombie until he came in, but she definitely tuned into him." Carl Addison ... Carl. It suddenly hit Connie. Fiona hadn't been trying to say *Connie* when she had briefly awakened; she'd been trying to say *Carl*. And the footprints on the path — two sets leaving the house, then dividing at the muddy edge of the gravel parking area — to get into opposite sides of the car? There was no sign of a struggle. Fiona had gone voluntarily. She knew Carl Addison, that much was clear, but ... how much did Ron know?

"We've got to get back up there right now!" said Connie, sliding along her side of the bench. They ran through the cafeteria toward the elevator — too slow — turning instead to the stairwell door. Connie could hear the echo of Alex and Jim's boots on the metal-edged stairs as she grabbed at the handrail, gasping with the effort of running up three flights of stairs. Coming through the doorway off the concrete stairwell landing, Connie skidded on the hallway floor, her shoulder hitting hard against the wall. She careened around the corner to room 412 as Jim and Alex charged the door. The sound of it crashing back against the wall reverberated through the hallway.

"No!" screamed Connie, as she grabbed the door frame to steady herself. She could see Ron Fortin wasn't even momentarily distracted by their entrance as he sprawled across Fiona's hospital bed, crushing the white pillow down on her face, shouting in rage as Alex and the sheriff struggled to pull him away from Fiona's thrashing body.

"He's dead, Fiona. I heard them talking about it in the ambulance. Now what're you going to do?" He twisted violently, trying to free himself from the hold Alex had on him while the sheriff handcuffed him, forcing him onto the other bed, face down.

Connie smoothed the bedding around Fiona before sinking back into the chair. Fiona's eyes opened slowly as if the light hurt her. Her head jerked toward Ron, and her body went rigid as she raised herself up on her elbow. "Why couldn't you just die and leave us alone?" she screamed. "You said you'd kill me if I ever tried to leave you. You'd hunt me down."

Fiona collapsed back against the pillow, her chest

heaving. "You must believe me, Connie. We had to kill him," she said as if it were the only reasonable solution.

Fiona sighed and continued in a soft, dreamy voice. "We thought he was dead. He should have been dead. Don't you think so, Connie?"

**

In the warmth of the breakfast room, Connie and Alex detailed the story for the Masseys as the four of them sat with mugs of coffee at the oak table. "What a day! Nothing could have prepared us for something like this happening in our own home," said Connie, passing the plate of scones and jam to Brad. "It's definitely not covered in the B&B guidelines."

"Isn't it ironic?" said Jenna, stroking Nacho, who was nesting chicken-style in her lap. "We came over to the Island to participate in a fantasy murder mystery, then find ourselves in the middle of a real murder plot starring your other guests."

"They're Jim's guests now," said Alex, putting his arm around Connie. "Who's for a walk on the beach, besides Talley? We don't want to waste an Island sunset."

Ebey's Landing
National Historical Reserve

The land of the Reserve means the same to me as it did to Coupeville pioneers. The Reserve is home. By celebrating the twentieth anniversary of the Reserve, we honor our connection to these people and to all that they accomplished in their time. I think they would be proud that we are keepers of this land in our time.

Early settlers traveled long and circuitous routes to arrive on Whidbey Island, as did many of us who came

Sandra McGillivray Ortgies   71

later. We arrived on the Island in 1992, following an Air
Force career which required moving every three to four
years. This move to Whidbey was different; it was our
choice. The move had to "feel right." Six years later, it still
feels right, and I wouldn't want to live anywhere else.

Most evenings my husband and I take a two-mile walk
across Sherman Road noting new plantings of age-old crops:
barley, squash, and beets. We continue up Cemetery Road
hill, where wild roses bloom among hedgerows first planted
in the 1800s. After pausing at Ebey's Prairie Overlook, we
circle around through Sunnyside Cemetery. The old family
names forge a bond with those of us who choose to settle
here too. From Arnold to Zylstra, the names on gravestones
are the same ones we see daily on local roads and
businesses.

When I look out on Penn Cove and see the Captain
Whidbey Inn's fifty-two-foot ketch *Cutty Sark* under full sail,
I can imagine Captain Thomas Coupe sailing his sloop
Maria into Penn Cove and Ebey's Landing over 125 years
ago.

On the opposite horizon I can watch a herd of black
and white Holsteins as "the girls" file across farm fields
against a backdrop of firs to their glacier-created grazing
hole by the new Kettles Trail. If conditions are right, Mount
Rainier appears between the Sherman barns.

Appreciation for these timeless scenes within the
reserve defines my days. I live here; this is my home.

On a Scale of ...

Tens and ones, exult and slam us
We yearn for nines and deal with twos
What's wrong with three through eight?
About a five I think, I like things smooth.

Five: Morning hugs in flannel sheets
       Gnarly bulbs in loam for April show

Rain patter on skylights while I read
Ideas that pounce and won't let go.

Fives are fulcrum choices, fanned out for us to take.
Grab the middle marker. You can call the play.

Time

Minutes glide together — waltzing partners — Strauss
    forever.
Years graze fields of poppies, pausing at
the highest ones, flashy reds and scorched earth
    patches.

So why is my calendar already paved?
Dance with me, the meadow's even.

Flagger Ahead

STOP!

Tanned, taut arms make jousting motions
and as we slow your flash smile softens the octagonal order.
Hot pine sap and tar fumes mingle with each gasp of air.
You've basted your face in zinc oxide, ignoring sweat
    trickling into a knotted bandana.
Your dust-layered "Redwings" like cartoon boots, too heavy
    for Leviskin legs.
Will it be today you'll have to fly into a ditch?
Is this why you twine a nest of wild roses round your hard
    hat?

❧

Jackie Griesinger

The Handicap

Hank drove his cart out of the shed and pulled up alongside Lou. "Ed's bringing another fellow to make up a foursome. Don't know him. A new member, I think." He took off his cap and smoothed his hand over his bald head before putting it back on. "Nice day," he said. "Just enough breeze to keep it cool."

"Yeah, glad we're not downwind from the dairy right now." Lou adjusted his dark glasses and fastened his golf bag onto the cart. "How're you doing today? How're the feet?"

"Well, they hurt like hell when I walk too much. But mostly I have to be careful if I start feeling woozy, and then I got my Snickers bars here in the basket in case I need one of them for a quick fix."

Lou turned in the direction of the steps crunching on the gravel, hearing Ed's slight limp and then Ed's voice making the introduction.

"Don, meet the other guys who'll be playing with us. Hank's there in the cart, and this is Lou."

Lou reached out for Don's hand with both of his, and said, "Glad to meet you, Don. Listen, I'll go on over to the first tee. I need to get a head start." He took off on foot with a long stride, Hank moving along behind him in his cart.

"Lou likes to walk," Ed explained when he saw Don watching the tall man moving down the slope. "Says he needs the exercise. Me, I'm looking at knee surgery in a few weeks, so I only hoof it when I have to."

"I'm not much for walking, either. I guess you can tell." Don patted his paunch. "I've put on a lot of weight since

my wife died, just lying around feeling sorry for myself." He
lifted his clubs next to Ed's on the cart, then took out a
handkerchief and blew his nose. "Allergies," he grunted,
turning his head as he pushed his bulk into the cart.

"It was my son who talked me into joining the country
club up here," he continued. "He thought I needed to get
out more, but I haven't played golf for a long time. Haven't
done much of anything, to tell the truth. I might not be very
good company."

"Just relax and enjoy the day," Ed said as he started his
cart. "I have to tell you, though, watch out where you step,"
he went on. "Damn Canadian geese settle in on the golf
course when they see these nice little lakes, and they leave
their crap all over the place. Sometimes you're in it before
you smell it."

The cart rattled over the gravel as they speeded up, and
Ed chuckled. "Matter of fact, one of the stupid male geese
must have had a thing for our resident swan. Was real mean
and wouldn't let any of the other geese near her. He even
chased the golfers away if any of us got too close."

"You're kidding, right?"

"No, that's a fact, so help me. Somebody should have
got a gun and shot that crazy old bastard. Come to think of
it, I haven't seen him around for a while. Maybe somebody
did."

Don looked at Ed, then decided it didn't matter if it was
the truth or not. It was a funny story. Maybe his son would
enjoy hearing about the mixed-up horny goose who tried to
romance a swan.

He changed the subject. "How often to you guys play?"

"Couple of times a week, usually. We like getting
outdoors when the weather's nice." Ed glanced overhead
and squinted into the brightness where a jet-trail was
zipping up the sky. "We mostly just play for the fun of it."
Then he nodded up the path to where Lou was
approaching the first tee. "Except maybe for Lou. You'll
find he's pretty quiet, and he takes his game a little more
serious, I guess. He's got a nice long drive, and his score is

Jackie Griesinger 75

lower than mine or Hank's. Frankly, I don't know how he does it."

"Practice?"

"Not really. More like blind luck, I'd say. But then, he hits the ball good, and all we have to do is spot it for him when it gets there." Then he laughed. "Actually, if you think about it, between the three of us, we make a whole person."

Ed's cart bumped along behind Hank's, and the sun shining through the branches made Appaloosa spots on the fairway. Douglas fir and hemlock lined the path on both sides, and willow trees thrived at the edge of the small lake in front of the first hole.

A cool September breeze blew through the sides of the vehicle, and Don took a deep breath. "Fresh-cut grass. They've just trimmed the greens." He relaxed against the seat. "Nice," he said.

When they had parked their carts, the men took turns teeing off. Ed made par, then Hank putted, and he and Lou bogeyed the par five hole. Don apologized for his double bogey when they marked their cards.

"Hell, none of us in this bunch ever apologizes for our game," Ed said, picking up his ball. "I don't even get mad anymore. It uses up too much energy, and at my age I need all the energy I can get. We just enjoy the activity and the fresh air, and then collapse in the clubhouse afterwards with some popcorn and a bottle of beer."

"I enjoy the fresh air, all right," Lou said, walking alongside. "But I'm still hoping someday I might play my age. You know, a 79. That means bringing my handicap down about four or five strokes."

"Fat chance of any of us making that kind of a score," Hank replied. "Of course the older we get, the better the possibilities."

"Yeah, that's right." Ed turned to Don as they went back to their cart. "One of our old-timers, name of John Berg, he's about ninety-three and still plays once in a while. I heard he shot a 93 not too long ago. Scored his age, but just about had a heart attack when he realized it."

"Well, you'd have to live that long and have a 23 handicap before that would work," Hank said.

When they drove down toward the second hole, a par three, the fairway stretched wide before them, with bunkers on either side of the green. There was no water to shoot across, and the ground was level for the first hundred yards or so, but the winking pattern of sunlight and shadows and the narrow archway through the trees to the pin was a challenge.

Ed pulled a tee out of his pocket and pushed it into the ground. "One hundred and seventy-eight yards," he muttered. "I'm going to try to get me another par."

He set the ball on the tee with a groan. "Damn knee," he grumbled as he swung the club. The ball curved low into the trees and came down not far from a tall pine. "Well, didn't get much distance on that one." He slammed his club into his golf bag.

Lou stepped up and set his ball on the tee and took out his three wood. He took a practice swing to loosen up. Then, looking out of the corner of his best eye, and with his head cocked to one side, he swung hard. His wood contacted the ball, and with a whack it arced  high and faded to the right. Then it bounced onto a rise just above the green. It rolled down the slope, leveled off, slowed, then hit the pin.

"It went in! I saw it. I'm sure it went in!" Don was jumping up and down, wheezing and waving his hat.

"Damned if it didn't." Hank nodded. "I saw it, too!"

"Hey, buddy, you made a hole-in-one! First one I ever saw!" Ed yelled, patting Lou on the back. "Not bad for a guy who's legally blind!"

Lou took off his dark glasses and squinted off toward the green. He smiled. "Well, what do you know about that? That ought to help my handicap!"

Geometry Lesson

A triangle, the three of us,
Three sides, not equal, really
Obtuse.
You, the long side, stretching.
He, holding on, grasping.
Me, the bottom line,
Always the bottom line.

You detached yourself from us both,
Then centered, invisible,
Almost.
Me, I found you, became
An orbit around your body,
A circular line
Attempting to enclose.

You felt too cramped, inhibited.
You evaded, changed your course,
Escaped,
Got outside my circle,
Then touched my circumference
As a tangent line
Meets at a special point.

Not satisfied, I needed more,
Struggled to encompass you
Again.
You pushed away, lost interest.
So now, we're equidistant,
Two parallel lines
Never touching,
Forever.

The Scent of Lilacs

Two o'clock. Exactly. Alexander looked at his Rolex again as he pushed himself out of his rented Mercedes into the hot California afternoon. It was only a little cooler under the canopy of the art gallery.

In his eagerness, he'd called from the airport, but it had been too early in the morning to talk to anyone. A remote and cultivated voice answered with clipped precision, almost as if it were a part of the answering machine itself.

"La Galleria will be open from two o'clock until nine-thirty this evening. Please leave a message at the beep."

So he would have to wait until two o'clock.

Alexander was almost fifty and he was tired. He was also pissed. This past week, he'd personally been to four galleries in New York, called the Stratford salon in London and the Fleur de Lis in Paris, made numerous inquiries, then flown to the Houston museum on a tip from another collector. None of the administrators had any of M'Lou's work, and hadn't for some time. At first he was more puzzled than angry at hearing things like, "Sorry, Mr. Dennison, we have none of the M'Lou paintings," or "No, we've had no word from her agent."

But now he was disturbed by the fact that nobody seemed to have any idea where she was. Alexander had kept track of her in a quiet way for many years, never wanting her to know his interest was anything more than that of a collector, even though the two of them had been friends from childhood.

He knew she had a small villa in Paris and an apartment in Manhattan, and that she occasionally slipped away to her uncle's lodge in the Rockies to work. That was when she painted most of her powerful snowscapes, soaring mountains and frozen lakes. One of these paintings was in his own collection: an avalanche with a lilac tree tumbling

Jackie Griesinger 79

down a cliffside between two huge boulders, with a brooding sky overhead.

"I'm going to be a famous artist and make lots of money," she had told him the day they graduated. They were sitting together on a campus bench, and she had pulled a long strand of hair under her chin and started to twist it the way she did when she was thinking about serious things. Then she said, "And I'll never come back."

He sighed. "Yeah, I know." Then he added, "Dad doesn't know where to send me to college. He says big as I am I should at least be able to play football, but I just can't get with that stuff. I d-don't think I'll ever really a-a-mount to anything. B-but I know you will, Mary Lou."

She'd taken his large hand in both of hers and looked into his eyes. "Denny, we're two of a kind in different ways, I think. You and I, we've been hiding for all these years, but this is our big chance to get away from it all. Let's do it!"

She stood up then and smiled. "Look, you may think you're the Incredible Hulk, but we both know you have the heart of an artist."

"Will you write to me?" he was finally able to ask, trying not to stammer.

"Of course, Denny. You're my knight in shining armor." Then she had walked away toward the park. It was June, and the lilac trees were in bloom.

He'd agreed to Yale, but insisted to his family that fine arts was what he wanted, and Mary Lou had gotten that wonderful art scholarship in New York. They'd written for a while, and he was able to get into the city to see her some weekends. His letters were long and informative, hers brief and rambling, and then they stopped.

Like now. Only he'd found her then, studying in Paris, after he'd gotten his degree and his father had died, leaving him with little self-esteem, but with loads of money.

This time, he knew she wasn't in Paris. Or New York. And there were no more relatives to call, at least he knew of none.

But he did remember her paintings of the wild Pacific

coastline, and decided to check for himself to see if she might be out there now. He'd taken a flight from Houston, and trusted his intuition that had led him to this exclusive seaside gallery in California.

He pushed open the large door with "La Galleria" etched into the heavy glass, and stepped into the quiet foyer of the building, closing out the boom of the waves against the rocky shoreline a short distance away. He paused a moment, brushed his sleeves, straightened his tie, then ran his hand over his chin. His hasty morning flight hadn't given him much time to work on the airplane rumple, and the quick shave in the car was barely adequate. Still, the well-tailored Armani suit gave him the confidence he needed to appear the sophisticated connoisseur he had become.

When he had opened another glass door, he found himself in a circular room with a modern kidney-shaped desk in the center. A telephone message machine monitored one end of the desk, and an arrangement of Bird-of-Paradise flowers in a silver vase kept an aggressive watch with their sharp beaks pointed as though daring any intruders to come any closer. A large leather-bound folder in the middle of the desk was the only other indication that the place might be open for business.

As if a silent bell had announced his entry, a small personage emerged from the hallway behind a concave wall. She was wearing a purple suit with a bright orange scarf at her throat. Her moussed hair was spiked across the top of her head, and her long pointed nose seemed to pull her forward as she walked toward the desk.

When she stood behind the vase, Alexander could scarcely repress a chuckle. She blended so perfectly with the flowers, she could have been a real Bird of Paradise quite at home in a tropical jungle.

Her eyes pierced him with an oblique gaze before acknowledging his presence with a question. "Ah, you must be Mr. Dennison? Won't you please sit down."

Alexander extended his personal card and then sat

Jackie Griesinger 81

down in front of the desk. "And you, I presume, are Miss Albares? I left a message this morning. I'm interested in obtaining a M'Lou." He paused, then went on. "For myself."

"Ah, yes. A M'Lou. Well." She sat on the edge of the desk chair and looked at his card. Then she said, "I'm afraid, Mr. Dennison, you are just about a day too late. We did have one of her paintings up until yesterday, but it is no longer available."

"Until yesterday, you say? Wh-what happened yesterday?' Alexander felt the words choking his throat. He leaned forward and took a deep breath. "What do you mean, 'no longer available'?"

"I'm sorry. We received an e-mail yesterday morning informing that the one painting we had in our gallery had been sold and requesting that it be sent to a certain address immediately. The bank wired a check, and we are getting it ready right now."

Alexander stood up. "It's still here? Which one?"

Miss Albares started to open the he folder on her desk. Then she said, "It's a self-portrait. An abstract, titled 'Echo No. 4.' It's one of her latest, and we are lucky to have had it here in our gallery. I'm sure you know the commission alone is — ."

"I m-must see it!" He started toward the hallway and turned. "Please, Miss Albares. This is very important to me."

She hurried after him as he strode around the corner. "Wait, Mr. Dennison. I'm not sure you'll be able to see it. It could be in the crate by now. The men were starting to —. Wait! Turn left up here. The workshop is behind these doors."

A man in coveralls was pounding nails in some wooden slats, and another was sliding a small painting into a padded crate.

She called out. "Just a minute, Jim. This gentleman would like to look at the painting before you pack it up."

Alexander took the framed picture and set it against a stack of boards. In the harsh fluorescent lighting, the brilliant splashes of raw color on the canvas formed a cruel conceptual image of a frightened face. Mary Lou's face, detached, disconnected from reality, portrayed by uncertain lines and angry thrusts of a broad brush. Alexander squinted into the painting, searching. Searching for the trademark that must be hidden somewhere, the lilac tree. And then he saw it, upside-down in the bosom of the figure, purple blossoms tumbling like confetti into the crevasse of her breast, grotesque branches reaching upward encircling her throat.

He backed away, his hand at his mouth, not able to speak.

"What is it, Mr. Dennison? I assumed you were familiar with her work. This abstract. You seem upset."

Alexander's words were harsher than he intended. "Miss Albares, if you can't give me the name of the buyer, you must tell me where this painting is being delivered."

"I'm sorry, Mr. Dennison. As I told you, the check came through the bank. I only know where the painting will be taken. But I'm not sure I am free to give you that information."

"Miss Albares, I-I think I know who bought this painting, but it's urgent that you tell me where it's going! I have reason to believe that M'Lou has bought this painting herself." He ducked his head, swallowed, and forced the words out. "Listen, I absolutely must know where you're sending it!"

Then, without waiting for an answer, he said, as if it would explain everything, "You see, I knew her. I knew M'Lou when she was just a little girl. When she was Mary Lou McKinney. We — ah — we grew up together."

"I see." Miss Albares sighed, then took his arm. "Mr. Dennison, why don't we look up the address in my files."

***

Traffic on the coast highway was sparse as Alexander drove north from Monterey, following the map. It was after three o'clock, and still unusually bright. The sun, glinting on the ocean below the cliffs, made him squint as he pounded

Jackie Griesinger

along the hot asphalt, approaching frequent puddles of wavering moisture that disappeared when he got closer.

The Mercedes almost drove itself, but his hands were tense on the wheel. Though the road coiled itself along the coastline, Alexander was able to give his thoughts to what he hoped to find at his destination. He was sure now that he would find Mary Lou, sure his instincts were correct. But why she was there concerned him. They'd been out of touch too long.

He remembered the last time he'd seen her. A gallery opening in New York, a year ago. It was an elite showing of some of her recent work, modern abstracts, some in the geometric lines of early Klee, but all strictly her own style. There were two untitled more loosely painted portraits in a vague outline technique that he had never seen before. Nightmarish faces they were, all with weird, gaping mouths, straggling hair like tree roots. He was frowning at them when he'd turned and seen M'Lou walk into the room.

She'd come in quietly and alone, and none of the other guests noticed her at first. She was wearing a long black dress with a beaded satin bolero, and her blonde hair, lightly streaked with gray, was pulled to one side in a heavy braid that fell over her left shoulder. Her only jewelry was a pair of gold loop earrings, and her lips were soft with just a bit of color.

Just then, there in the car when he thought back to that moment when she started across the room toward him, he felt like a large fist had punched him in the chest, and he realized for the first time how much he loved her, had always loved her.

He stepped hard on the gas, and the car speeded forward.

He hadn't even forgotten the crazy sentence she spoke to him as they stood beside each other that night. "Abstract art is a product of the untalented, sold by the unprincipled to the utterly bewildered," she had said. "Al Capp said that, did you know?"

He looked down at her and then at the portraits. "Al

Capp's a cartoonist. What made you say that?"

"These paintings are cartoons. Don't you get it, Alexander? I'm painting cartoons now, and nobody can tell the difference!" A convulsive laughter shook her shoulders until she stopped abruptly and covered her mouth. "Sorry, but it's all just so funny. Such a game. Skip to my Lou."

He had been alarmed, even back then. But all he said was that he had never liked abstracts. Now he wished he'd paid more attention to her mood.

"But you do understand them, my paintings, don't you, Alexander?" She had grasped his sleeve. "All of them? You understand why I've painted the lilac tree into every picture?"

"I'm probably the only one who does understand. Everybody else thinks it's a gimmick, or a trademark," he said. "Your agents, your clients and buyers. And it's worked for you, made your work mysterious, unique — and of course, expensive." He took a glass of champagne from a passing waiter and handed her one. Then he added, "I expect I might be the only person in the world who does know."

With her free hand she reached up to her shoulder and began to twist the braid. "No, Alexander. Remember, one other person knew about the lilac tree. But you're the only one who ever cared."

Alexander's thoughts had intruded into his memory so profoundly that he almost missed the sign at the intersection. He braked the car and turned the wheel onto the road leading into a small village. He found himself driving along a well-kept street lined with adobe shops and windmill palms.

The note he had stuck to the mahogany dashboard had the scribbled instructions that Miss Albares had given him, and he drove on through the town and turned left, following a more secluded but well-kept route, with shrubs and plants along the embankments. Two miles later, he found himself driving again along the edge of the ocean, and then, as he came around a bend, an ornate sign standing in the center of a huge bed of poppies announced his destination. "The Palisades."

As he drove up the long curved drive, an expanse of green lawn on the left, and the long wood and stucco building up ahead to the right, Alexander noted how isolated the place was. He never would have been able to find it without the precise instructions, and it was no wonder his search for M'Lou had been so complicated. "Lord," he thought. "What the hell was she doing in this place? If she was here."

But then, after he'd seen that last painting at "La Galleria," he knew she had to be here, and also why she was here. He prayed he wasn't too late.

He parked the Mercedes in a small parking lot that was marked "Visitors," discreetly surrounded by a well-trimmed hedge. The air was hot and oppressive, and by the time he hurried across the broad patio to the large oak doors of the main building, his silk shirt was sticking to his skin under his jacket.

But once he'd opened the doors and gone inside, the cold from the air conditioner took him by surprise, and he caught his breath. The room was dim, and it was a few seconds before he found he was in a lobby with huge ferns hanging from high-beamed ceilings, and in the center, a clay fountain splashed gently into a stone pool.

Alexander looked around. "My God, where is everybody?" he said aloud. His footsteps on the flagstones sounded an angry staccato as he walked toward an opening behind the fountain.

Just then, a man appeared wearing Dockers and a blue short-sleeved shirt open at the neck. Blond hair contrasted nicely with the tanned face and the perfectly flossed alabaster smile. "Hello, sir. Sorry I didn't get up here sooner. I just glanced away from the monitor for a few minutes. I'm Bob Logan. Can I help you?"

It was then Alexander noticed the two small cameras tucked discreetly into the opposite walls of the lobby. He didn't much like being watched. It made him feel uncomfortable.

"I hope so," he answered. "I'm looking for Miss McKinney."

The young man looked bewildered, so Alexander said, "Maybe Mary Lou McKinney, or just M'Lou? The artist?"

"Ah, M'Lou!" He seemed relieved and frustrated at the same time. "Well, and what was your name, sir?"

Alexander felt his heart jump under his vest pocket as he pulled out his card. When he handed it to the young man, he felt, for the first time, that he really was on the right track. "Look," he said, "I've come a long way, and I've pretty much been all over the country trying to find her. Who do I have to talk to to get some answers?"

"Please, Mr. Dennison," Logan said. "Let me take you into our lounge, and I'll see if Dr. Van Giesen is available."

Alexander paced the floor, checking his watch every five minutes. When the doctor finally entered the lounge, Alexander noted that he was close to his own age, but tall and slim, and, like Logan, was dressed casually.

The doctor spoke with a faint European accent when he asked Alexander to sit down.

"I believe we should talk together, you and I, Mr. Dennison. Your card tells me your name, but nothing about you, or, exactly who you are. I need to know why you wish to see — M'Lou."

"Is she here?" Alexander tried to keep his voice calm.

"Mr. Dennison, one thing at a time. This is a very private clinic. People don't walk in here and make demands to see our patients unless we know exactly who they are and what they want. In fact, many of the people in our care don't particularly wish to see anyone. I'm sure you understand that."

"I do, Doctor, and I'm really not a rude man. But the thing is, if she's here, I am positive that she wants — no, needs — to see me. If she's as desperate as I think she is, I don't want another day to go by without seeing her, talking to her. Please, can't you help? Just tell her that Denny is here. I'm absolutely positive that she'll want to see me."

Jackie Griesinger 87

Van Driesen looked at Alexander long moments before he answered. Finally, he said, "Right now, M'Lou is here. At least part of the time it's M'Lou." He paused. "Now, tell me about you and Mary Lou."

Alexander took a deep breath and began to talk, slowly at first, not knowing where to start. He decided to think back to their early school days. "I was big for my age, never seemed to fit in with kids in my class, or even my folks, for that matter." He gazed out into the garden bright with hibiscus and emerald shrubs. "After school, I used to go and sit in the park by myself, no good at any of the usual school sports, and I never wanted to go home too soon because my dad was always after me about stuff like that."

The doctor nodded. "And you and Mary Lou were friends?"

"Mary Lou and I started first grade together, and even then, when she was only six, I knew she was wonderful, the way she could make such fanciful drawings with just crayons. Art was my favorite subject, too." He laughed at that. "Though I couldn't draw, I loved the idea of depicting ideas in color, and Mary Lou was, I don't know, exceptional, even at that age."

He got up and walked to the window. "At first though, I couldn't figure out why she always put a lilac tree in all her drawings."

He loosened his tie and took a deep breath. "When I was ten and she was nine, I used to find her under this big kind of bushy old lilac tree in the back end of the park. She'd be curled up in a little ball, her face streaked with dirty tears, and clutching a ragged lilac bloom in her fist. Sometimes she'd be rocking back and forth singing that crazy song, you know, 'Skip to My Lou.' Just that one verse, though, the one that says, 'I'll find another one, prettier than you.'"

Alexander shook his head. "I didn't know why then, but it was like she was singing a prayer that he would find someone else, prettier than she was. It was only later, when I took her to our guest house to help her get cleaned up, that she told me about the bastard."

Dr. Van Driesen nodded. "I've heard her singing the song. And I suspected it was someone in the family. Please, go on."

Alexander set his jaw and scowled. "I hated him. He treated Mary Lou's mother pretty bad, too. I knew she knew, but she was too scared of him to do anything about it, of course. I wished I could kill him, or put him in jail, or something, but I was just a kid. I didn't know what to do, and Mary Lou made me promise not to tell anyone."

The doctor said, "This is helpful, hearing this from you. Is there more?"

Alexander shrugged. "By the time Mary Lou was fourteen, he seemed to lose interest, and she never mentioned him after that. But I know it's always been there in her head. I've never spoken to anyone about this before."

He sighed. "After that, her teacher got her a scholarship and Mary Lou followed her star." He swallowed hard and stared at the floor. "Today, though, in a gallery down in Monterey, I saw one of her recent paintings, an abstract. It really scared me. It was a self-portrait, and the roots of the lilac tree, it looked to me, were literally choking the life out of her."

Van Driesen leaned forward. "Yes, the lilac tree. You know about the tree, I believe. Why it was in her head, in her art?"

"I-I always knew, from the day I found her in the park, that the tree had been a symbol of safety to her, but when she painted it in such a menacing way, that told me something different was going on. I was afraid she might do, or be thinking about doing, something desperate. That's why I got here as fast as I could, because I was sure she was the one who bought it, and that I'd find her here."

He stood up. "She is here, isn't she?"

Dr. Van Driesen stood and took his arm. "Come with me, Mr. Dennison. I spoke with her when Mr. Logan told me who you were and why you're here. I'll take you to her."

"Is she okay?"

Jackie Griesinger 89

"She's very busy right now. She's been painting for several days."

They went outside and walked along a shaded path toward a white stucco bungalow. Alexander could scarcely control his anxiety as they reached the house. The doctor knocked on the door and called in. "Mary Lou, it's Dr. Van Driesen. I've brought your visitor." He turned to Alexander, and for the first time, he smiled. "I'm sure it's Mary Lou that's here this afternoon, at least it will be after she sees you. She might want to show you why she's been painting so much lately. Go on in." He pushed open the door and then turned and walked back toward the main building.

Alexander stepped inside to a cluttered room, bright with late afternoon sun that shone through sliding glass patio doors. Mary Lou was there, wearing a paint-spattered smock and holding a brush in her hand. An easel stood in front of her, the painting on it catching the light. She dropped the brush and walked toward him.

"Denny," she said. "Oh, my God, I'm so glad you found me!" She came close to him and looked up into his face.

"You must have known I'd find you. I always did," he said, when he could talk. He pulled her into his arms and laid his cheek against the top of her head. Never in their lives had they ever been so close, like this. She didn't push away, and even though she smelled like turpentine and paint, he didn't care. He held her tight for a minute and then asked, "Are you all right? I've been worried about you."

She turned and said, "Come and see what I'm doing. I've been busy for several weeks now."

She led him to her easel where one of her seascapes had been set. He stooped down and looked closely at it. He thought he knew the painting, the waves dashing on the shore, the moonlit sand, the foamy spray. But where was the lilac tree growing out of the rocks, with its purple petals drifting out over the water?

"There's no lilac tree here. I know this painting, but there's no lilac tree."

She walked around the room where many of her other paintings were leaning against the wall and propped against each other.

"No, Denny, no more lilac trees. I've painted them all out. There'll be more of my work coming in here, from galleries and museums, the ones that aren't sold. My agent's been sending them to me."

Mary Lou looked out the window. "I hardly remember doing the most recent portrait of myself, but I knew when I painted roots grasping at my throat that I needed help. I could even smell the lilacs. It was like the canvas was filled with the scent of them. That's when I got in touch with Dr. Van Driesen."

Alexander bit his lip. "Yes. I saw that painting today, Mary Lou. I-it scared me. That's why I'm here."

She turned and smiled at him. "I'm not worried any more. Dr. Van Driesen says I'm going to be fine now. At least I'll be almost a whole person again, now that I know why I painted the way I did, and the things I painted."

"I always knew," Alexander said.

"I know you did. But let me show you why I don't need the lilac tree to hide under any more."

She went to a small table and took out an envelope and handed it to him. "It's from my mother."

He unfolded it. It was a letter, posted from Oregon, dated three weeks earlier. The note, in large scrawly letters, was brief. It read, "MARY LOU YOUR STEP-FATHER DIED YESTERDAY. THOUGHT YOU WOULD LIKE TO KNOW. MOM."

He put the paper down and walked over to the work she had stacked up along the walls, the canvasses where she had painted out all the lilac trees. When he had looked them all over carefully, he said, "Let's walk down toward the ocean and watch the sunset."

She took his hand and they went across the lawn to a bench overlooking the water.

Neither of them spoke for a while. The light breeze puffed wisps of her hair across her face as they watched the

Jackie Griesinger 91

fading sun color the waves below.

Finally he turned to her and said, "Mary Lou, now that you've taken out all the lilac trees, I'm afraid your paintings are pretty, well, pretty ordinary."

She looked at him and smiled. "Yes, I know. Isn't it wonderful?"

Point/Counterpoint

Breathe deeply, smell the rain,
The crystal damp, cool beads.
Smell the mist,
Salty tears.

Breathe deeply, smell the sea,
The stinging spray, wet sand.
Smell the clam,
Empty shell.

Breathe deeply, smell the woods,
The mossy bough, dry leaves.
Smell the pine,
Rotting log.

Breathe deeply, smell the rose,
The garden bloom, bouquet,
Smell the myrrh,
Embalming oil.

❧

Helen Gleghorn

Jack

Iwas startled awake by the telephone ringing on my night stand. A little fearful, I reached for the telephone in a sleepy haze.

"Hello."

"This is the nurse at Hillcrest Hospital in Tulsa, Oklahoma. May I speak to Helen Gleghorn?"

"This is she," I answered.

"You were listed as next of kin for Murray Jack Leake. He passed away at 2:30 A.M."

I gasped. My body trembled. Tears welled up in my eyes. I could hardly talk. The nurse said, "I need the name of a mortuary to send his body."

It had been thirty years since the last time I was in Tulsa. "I need your number. I have to make a call." The number was given. I hung up the telephone. I began to cry. I was the last one of my family alive. I looked at my wristwatch. The time was 3 A.M.

In the living room my address book contained the number of Jack's stepdaughter, Jenny, who lived in Tulsa. I dialed, and after many rings Jenny answered sleepily.

"Jen, this is Jack's sister, Helen. Do you remember me?"

"Oh, yes, Helen. It's been a long time hearing from you."

I said, "I just received a call from Hillcrest Hospital saying Jack passed away at 2:30 A.M."

Jen said, "Oh, Helen, I'm so sorry. I knew Jack wasn't taking his high blood pressure medication."

"Jen, I need the number of a mortuary to have Jack sent. Could you get the name and telephone number for me?"

Jen said, "Yes, Helen. I will call you right back. What's your telephone number?"

Click went the telephone. My mind raced. I wondered if

he had a will? We weren't too close, only sending cards at Christmas and birthdays. In a call from about a month ago, he had mentioned that if anything happened to him, there was to be no funeral.

I came out of the daze, hearing the ring of the telephone. It was Jen.

"I have the name for you, Helen. I wrote it down," Jen said. "When you called, I was shocked. I didn't tell you Jack was found yesterday laying on the floor. He fell and broke his hip and had an aneurysm. I didn't have your telephone number. I usually check on him. I called for two days. No answer. The manager of the apartment found him on the floor. He was there two days."

I began to cry, thinking of my brother all alone. "Thanks, Jen. I will get back to you."

I called the hospital. A chaplain answered. I told him who I was and gave him the telephone number of the mortuary. He consoled me. I thanked him and hung up. The time was 6 A.M.

The mortuary called to say they had received the body. They quoted prices for embalming and cremation. I chose cremation. I would have to give them his U.S. Army serial number to file for permission to bury him in a national cemetery. I didn't have the information, but would send it later. There was to be no funeral, as Jack had requested.

After the telephone call, I became so angry at my brother. Leaving all the details for me to handle. I knew he was on Medicaid. I wondered if he had a bank account. Jen was in bad health, but she had a son who could go through his possessions. Jen had mentioned that Jack kept important papers and other things in a foot locker. It was bad enough that I had lost my brother, without the burden of settling his estate, burial, and expenses.

Evening approached. The telephone rang. It was Jen. "Helen, I went through all the information he had in his foot locker. There was no will. He had a bank account of $150. I found his Army serial number. His rent was paid to the first of the month. I know you will have the expense for burial. We could sell his furniture for you, to help some."

"Oh, Jen, thank you for your help. All I want is the foot locker with his medals and pictures, etc."

"I can do that. It will take a few days to get everything done. I'll keep in touch," Jen said.

I called the mortuary. When they answered, I gave them Jack's serial number so they could process the forms for burial in a national cemetery. The nearest cemetery was Fort Gibson National Cemetery, about 150 miles from Tulsa. The fee for taking Jack there would be $50. I said I would be responsible for the cost. "Thank you," I said, and hung up the telephone. Since I was on a limited income myself, I would have to take the money out of my savings. I couldn't let him be buried as a pauper. I was always the big sister that took care of him when he was little.

A week later Jen called to say she had sold the furniture and would mail me the foot locker. I thanked her again, saying I would keep in touch.

A month later I received a letter from the national cemetery saying they had received Jack's remains, with a map showing his burial site. Two weeks later I received his foot locker with medals and pictures.

I opened the locker. I took out his medals. I remember he shared an experience in Korea, in battle. His platoon assaulted a hill. All were killed except my brother. He had a ramrod posture all his life from service duty.

Another picture showed Jack as a caddie on the golf course to earn money during his teen years. There was a picture of his wedding day, of Rosalie, his wife.

On and on, more memories to recall. All that was left of a man's life and my memories.

ح

Suzanne Fulle

Legacy

The noon whistle on the Pickle Factory blew as Belinda and Marianne came down the street in front of the old brick building. The two girls stopped to look up at the clock stuck like the eye of Cyclops in the center of its forehead. It was odd to see the clock up close like this. The family usually told the time by reading the clock from the balcony through the sweetgum trees with Grandpa Goody's old spyglass. The family hadn't had a clock since the depression started, and now it was 1939.

"I wish I'd get a Mickey Mouse watch for my birthday." Belinda swatted at a fly on her bare leg but missed.

"I don't." Marianne waited patiently. "I want a Shirley Temple like the other girls have."

"You always want to be a girl." Belinda was disgusted. The only thing that kept her from being totally in despair about being a girl was that if she were a boy, that would mean there would be an uneven number on each side of the family. Already there were two boys, big brother Robbie and baby Peter. She and Marianne were holding their own on the feminine side.

And if Roosevelt got the U.S. in the war, and it went on until she grew up, she'd have to go and fight. Aunt Cissy was always going on about how near Robbie was getting to fighting age, and he was only fifteen.

Belinda was ten, so it would be eight years before she had to go, but it would be only three for Robbie. Marianne, who was eight, and baby Peter, who was one, were too little to worry about.

"Robbie said there are baby alligators in that washtub by the fence." Marianne held back. Then she frowned as Belinda immediately went over toward it. "I knew I shouldn'ta mentioned it!"

They peered down at three small alligators, about the size of large tadpoles. The alligators looked so helpless that Belinda almost picked one up, until it opened its mouth and a row of tiny white teeth shone in the noon sun. She jerked her hand back.

"Wonder if they got them down at Galveston?" Marianne gazed down at the babies. The ribbon on her sun hat had come untied. It hung down and the little alligators went back and forth under it. Marianne stepped back.

"Probably in some of those ditches." Belinda started back to the sidewalk. "You remember that time when we went crabbing with Daddy, he said Texas has as many alligators as Louisiana, but we don't brag about it like they do.

"We better get on home. Mama'll be worried about what happened to us."

There was no shade now on the sidewalk, and the two girls walked with their heads down, looking at their feet. Maybe they should carry Mama's old parasol, but they'd lost it three times already. Aunt Cissy said it was too valuable to be left in every five-and-dime in Texas.

Mama spied them from the back porch where she stood, dish towel in hand, talking to Elnora, the ironing woman. The slap of Elnora's black feet on the old porch drowned out what Mama said at first.

"Girls! Hurry! Robbie's coming home for lunch," the girls finally heard Mama. "Get my thread?"

With a groan, the girls got up from the lawn glider and joined the two women on the back porch. Belinda handed Mama the small brown bag with the spool of No. 60 white thread and flopped into Grandpa Goody's wicker chair. On the table there was a blue plate with peanut butter sandwiches and glasses of lemonade in dark blue Shirley Temple glasses.

Mama turned to Elnora, who set the iron on its haunches on the ironing board with a thud. "Will you be able to do some ironing early next week, Elnora? I'd like to have everything ready when Cousin Keith comes over from New Orleans."

"Yes'm. I understand that feeling. But I'm hepping Miz Olson on Monday, and I've got plans for Tuesday." Elnora took a sandwich from the blue willow plate and sat down on the back steps beside Marianne. "They's having a birthday party for Lee Ann Hofstein, and I'se to serve."

A birthday party at the Hofsteins'! They were the people who owned the picture show where the girls and Robbie went on Saturday afternoons.

Belinda stopped eating and gazed over at Marianne. Marianne's wide brown eyes welled with longing.

"What'll they have, Elnora?" Belinda begged. "Have you been to one before?'

Elnora laughed. "Yes'm! Lots of times. They's got so many kids, they's always having birthdays. Always something special. One time they had Mandrake the

Magician, and he cut one of them little boys right in two. Boy, did that little boy scream!

"This time I heah they's having a dog and pony show. Yessuh! A man gone come in and show an act. I tole George about it, and as big as he is, he plans to come by. I reckon Miz Hofstein can find something for him to do.

"I heah this may be the Hofsteins' last shindig. Miz Hofstein done told me they need every dime to get their folks out of Germany! You know, them Jews is really having a hard time over theah. I doan know but what we oughta collect something up for them, too. We sure have lots of calls on us these days."

"Elnora!" Mama cautioned. "Let's talk of happier things. No use adding our depression to the country's! Tell us about the party."

Elnora leaned back against the post. "Well, they certainly does theirselves proud. You know, they's picture people – they even had Jane Withers one time at their house. I seen a picture of them with her."

"Oh," Belinda sighed. It was just too much. Think of that hallowed yard. Think of mixing with theater people! All those beautiful children, dressed in flower colors, weaving beautiful maypoles. Belinda could just see the little Hofstein children skipping around the flower bedecked pole, weaving long garlands of roses and ivy onto a tall pole carved with cupids. She'd seen one like it at the May Fete at the school. "It's simply not fair! Some people have all the luck!"

***

It was after dark when Robbie came home. Elnora had finished the ironing. It hung stiff, smelling of starch, on the screened porch. Elnora waved goodbye and hurried off down the street to Shady Acres just as the pickle factory clock chimed six o'clock.

Robbie was too tired to eat when he came into the dining room. His hair was curly with perspiration as he slumped in his chair.

Suzanne Fulle 99

"Robbie! I thought you were coming home for lunch! How could you stay so late? Weren't you hungry?" Mama moaned as she put an orange bowl full of rice and chili on the table. "Why don't you just come home when you hear the whistle? It doesn't matter what Daddy says!"

"He didn't tell me to stay." Robbie poked his fork, at the rice that Mama served him, but didn't take a bit. That was unusual. Rice and chili beans was a great favorite.

Mama bit her lip and went into the kitchen for lemonade. She wasn't really mad, Belinda knew. She just looked like that when she looked at Robbie. Belinda had heard her talking to Daddy in the middle of the night.

"Robert, he's just too young for so much work! Fifteen! He does a man's job and more. Why, he never has time to do anything with his friends, working for you days, and now this night job at the library! I was so hoping he could take it a little easier this summer in the heat. You know he's growing so fast!"

Daddy had answered in his tired voice, "He's lucky to have a job these days. And anyway, I don't insist he come down to the factory. I'm not saying he doesn't take a lot off my shoulders. The men like him. But now that I've had to let so many go, there's only Arnie left. We need every bit of help we can get."

"Oh, Robert! Is this what we planned for our eldest son? Couldn't I come down and help?"

"You're practically running a boarding house now! This depression won't last forever. Roosevelt'll quit tinkering and we'll come out of it. Robbie's all right. He's got a good strong constitution. I'll keep an eye on him."

Belinda knew what kind of eye Daddy kept on Robbie.

The phone rang now and Marianne answered. "Robbie, it's for you."

Belinda followed Robbie to the phone. Whenever he was home, she was always there. He didn't seem to mind, but sometimes he fell asleep when she was talking.

"Yeah, Rex? Tuesday? Well, maybe. I'll let you know. Thanks ... oh ..." Robbie held out the phone to Mama, who

100   *Beneath the Rain Shadow*

was going by with an armload of wash. "Rex's mother wants to talk to you."

Mama took the phone in surprise. Marianne came in and clung to the banister.

"Why, yes, Mrs. Hofstein. Why, I don't know." Here she turned and gazed at the girls. "Well, I suppose so. That would be lovely. Why, thank you so much."

She hung the receiver back on the wall.

"What is it? What is it?" Belinda and Marianne jumped down to grab Mama's arm. "What did she want? What did she say?"

"She wanted to know if you all would like to come to the party with Robbie. No one is bringing presents, but I think you might take one of those teapots that you got two of for Christmas."

"Oh. To the party!"

"Well, what do you think, Robbie? Would you take the girls with you?"

"Oh, please Robbie! Please!" They clung to his arms and hugged him until he finally laughed. Then they dragged him down on the rug with them and began fighting to kiss him, while he covered his face with his hands and pretended to hate it.

Aunt Cissy led baby Peter through the door. Peter toddled over and climbed on top of the pile.

"Well, this is certainly ladylike!" Aunt Cissy's eyebrows met her gray hairline.

Mama leaned down and picked up Peter with one hand and pulled Belinda up with the other. "They've been invited to the Hofstein's birthday party."

"Jews," Aunt Cissy sniffed.

Belinda made a face at Aunt Cissy. Aunt Cissy always thought there was something wrong with everything they did. Too bad they needed her check so much. "You're just hateful!" Belinda glared at her aunt.

"Belinda," Mama warned, then she turned to her sister. "I know you don't care for them, but I will not let you talk like that here." Mama hurried on as Aunt Cissy straightened

Suzanne Fulle

herself up. "And Robbie probably wouldn't make the effort to go at all without the girls. You know how he is. I want him to have some fun. See his friends a little."

"Well, if you don't care what sort of friends he has." Aunt Cissy's voice was softer. If it was good for Robbie, it was all right with Aunt Cissy.

Tuesday dawned clear and cool. Belinda danced in to breakfast singing, "It didn't rain! It didn't rain!"

Grandpa Goody looked up from the breakfast table where he sat reading the newspaper. He leaned over and pulled back the limp marquisette curtain. He peered at the dying grass and the limp strings of ivy on the brick wall. "I guess it didn't, at that."

"Though why you worried about rain after a solid month of drought." Mama shook her head as she dipped day-old bread into sweet batter and dropped it into the big iron skillet.

"Oh! *Pan perdu!*" Marianne squealed, racing into the room and collapsing into a chair. "Doesn't it smell gorgeous!"

The party was at four o'clock, but long before that time, Marianne and Belinda sat starched and ironed on the window seat. Belinda leaned down and pulled her ribbed white stockings higher on her skinny ankles. Marianne did the same.

"Don't move yours around so much," advised Belinda. "You'll get the paint off-center."

Marianne's socks were so full of holes that Belinda painted under each hole with white shoe polish. Wait until Aunt Cissy found that out.

"Do you think it'll show?" Marianne worried.

"Don't be silly." But Belinda wasn't really sure herself. She wasn't worried about the holes in her socks. What really bothered her was the hem of her skirt where Mama had let it out. Even Elnora had said when she ironed it yesterday, "Maybe we oughter sew some ric-er-rac around it."

Maybe those little Hofsteins and their theater friends would look down on the Bledsoes in last year's clothes.

"Oh, Lord," Belinda prayed, "when I get big, let me be rich. It's OK if you don't want to wait that long."

At last it was time to go.

Robbie loped down the stairs, pulling at the cuffs of his white shirt. His hair stood up in wet peaks and water glistened on his face.

Aunt Cissy went up behind him and smoothed his hair. Then she turned to straighten Belinda's collar and retie the bow in Marianne's blond hair.

"Off you go," she said.

Mother hugged Peter in her arms as she gazed at them. "Aren't the children growing up?" she murmured. "I want to remember them just like this."

They walked down the hot street in silence, staying in the shade of the sweetgum trees as much as they could. Their sun hats shaded their eyes. At each corner, they ran through the white hot sun to the safety of the shade trees on the other side.

They reached the boulevard and could see the Hofstein house set back from the road in a nest of mimosa trees.

Belinda threw her head back and felt herself ready for anything, any dazzle, any brilliance at the party.

"Look, there's Elnora in the kitchen." Marianne pointed up at the kitchen window as the three crossed the street and walked down the drive to where they could hear voices and see streamers tied to the fence posts.

Belinda held her clown-head teapot out before her like the head of John the Baptist.

I'll sure be glad to get rid of this, she thought. Can you imagine getting two of these for Christmas?

"Where should we go, Robbie?" Marianne held onto Belinda's skirt.

Robbie led the girls into a crowd of children who surrounded a small blue wagon and a goat and a perspiring man in a clown's suit. Then Robbie disappeared into the library with Rex.

From that moment until later when Belinda sat with Marianne in the grape arbor waiting for refreshments, the

Suzanne Fulle 103

time swept by for Belinda.

"This is the way it is," she breathed. "This is the way it really is. This is the way it will be for me when I grow up."

And now, here came Elnora and her son George, with big trays of birthday ice cream, cupcakes like little clowns, lemonade, paper clown hats, napkins, everything.

"Oh," Belinda and Marianne sighed together.

All the children sat on benches and gliders and swings and lawn chairs as Elnora and George served each one. After forever, Elnora and George came to the grape arbor where Belinda and Marianne waited like small garden statues.

"Hi, Elnora!" They giggled.

"What ... what chu Bledsoes doing heah?" Elnora froze before them.

"Why, why, we ... we were invited!"

"Heah? Ain't your Mama got any sense? Any pride? Heah? With people lak these?"

"What, what do you mean? What's the matter with them?" Belinda looked wildly at the groups of children, the blues and pinks and whites, the swirl of colors.

"What is it, Elnora?" Belinda's lips quivered. "Robbie's here!"

"Hit doan matter bout him," Elnora hissed, leaning closer. "Robbie's er boy! But you're ladies. You doan belong in a place lak this! Now git on home!"

She put the tray down on the wicker table and took each girl by the arm.

"No! No! Leave me alone!" Belinda said between clenched teeth, trying to jerk free.

But it was no use. Elnora's arms were like a vise. And Belinda couldn't bear that anyone might see or hear this.

"What's the matter with you, Elnora!" Belinda hissed, while Marianne sobbed quietly into her napkin. "Mother said we could come!"

"I doan care! She jest so far down with all these worries, she done forget herself. She know full well wat's fitten — and you Bledsoe girls ain't coming to no Jew house lak this.

I got ma standards!"

She pulled the girls to their feet and turned to George, who stood in the archway.

"George, you walk them home. Ah'll tell Miz Hofstein they took sick. An you high-tail yoself right back heah again to help."

Belinda's face was purple. "Elnora, you're as bad as Aunt Cissy! You're just — you're just old-fashioned!"

Elnora straightened Belinda's hat. "Now, stop that sassin', Belinda. My mind hit's made up."

It was no use. Belinda looked around at the other children talking happily as they ate the refreshments. It was no use. Even if she kicked and screamed. Some things were not to be.

"What about Robbie?" Belinda whispered.

"Ah'll explain to him. Ah'll explain to yo Mama. Ah'll explain to everyone in this whole wide world. You jest git on home, where you belong. Lan's sakes, Miss Belinda, Honey. What chu think Ah'm working for?"

Kaye LaTorra Erickson

Company's Coming

They're coming. Relatives. Should I change the sheets on the guest bed? They've only been slept on once. I flip, smooth and tuck.

Let me think. This is Bev. She's the one who will want the old family albums to remember through. I don't think I have even unpacked them.

No, no. Bev. She's the one who helps in the kitchen. That calls for cleaning the silver drawer and the utensil drawer. Get the dead celery out of the hydrator. Bleach the dish towels. Toss the pot-holder with the spaghetti sauce on it. Get rid of those stained dishrags. Open a new package. They look too new. Run them through the washer with the towels.

Get a haircut. No time, just trim the back a bit.

Vacuum. Dust the baseboards. Put out the bowl they gave us. She always asks if I ever use it.

Pick some pansies. Damn — slugs been at them. And I need to use up some of the rhubarb. Rampant. Leaves look like a jungle. Wonder if they like rhubarb. Make a pie. That custard one with the eggs.

No, I think they are into cholesterol. Forget the pie. What'll I cook? Fresh Penn Cove mussels. With garlic butter. Sure, with drinks, then salmon on the grill and some new potatoes. Breakfast? Waffles and strawberries. Such an unexpected visit. Probably only staying overnight. Maybe I can get a haircut before I shop.

Nope — no time. Damn — I wish they had given me a day or two. Well. Need some bourbon. Stop at the liquor store. Tom drinks lots of bourbon as I recall. He talks less and less about the greenhouse effect and the environment with each shot. Thank heavens. Start the ice-maker.

How will we entertain them? Take them to the rhododendron gardens. Then the waterfront, if it isn't raining. Jeez, I hope we can fill the time tomorrow. Wonder when they are leaving?

They said they would be here around three o'clock. Puff. I think we are ready for them. Hair a bit shaggy. Wow, those baseboards are pretty bad. Forget it. Remember the bifocals. Quit fussing. They probably got lost. It's only four-fifteen.

"Hi, you found us."

"Sorry we are late. We found these wonderful rhododendron gardens on the way up. Tom just had to stop."

Hugs and kisses. She had the bifocals on. Tom has lost some weight.

"About twenty pounds," he says. "Quit drinking. New man. No pollution in this body. Gotta take care of your own environment."

Bev says she likes my new hairdo but feels I look younger with it a bit shorter. They like the house. Bev takes off her glasses as she looks around. I start the steamer.

Yes, mussels. A specialty on the island. Allergic to shellfish. I didn't know he was. Oh, something new. Maybe polluted beaches. And you don't care for them either. Don't like that mushy stuff in the middle. Turn off the steamer and start fixing crackers and cheese. Cholesterol. Yes, I know about cheese. Just Seven-up for Tom, and you too. We'll all have Seven-up.

Start the barbecue. You do eat salmon. Bev fixes the potatoes. Gets lots of utensils out of the neat drawers. I do the salad. Tom tells us about the spotted owl and how important it is to the whole world. No, they don't have them in Arizona. It's lizards they protect. No. No trees. Just cactus.

You want to see the yard. I know I should use the rhubarb. Pie? Tom's favorite. With the eggs. Tom says the acid in the rhubarb kills the cholesterol in the eggs.

The family albums? I'll try to find them. Of course they are important to me. I just don't have a place for them. On the coffee table at your house. I thought that was Mary. You follow her example. Family is important. Like the environment. Of course it is.

Oh, don't apologize. You must be tired. Go ahead and turn in. And, Bev, how long will you be staying? Four days. No, no. Not too long at all.

We listen to the 10 P.M. weather report. Rain and heavy overcast through the weekend. Listen to the rain as it dances on the skylight. Teasing. I confess about the used guest sheets. We open the bourbon.

You Call This Progress?

I support the ERA in all its glory.
I don't mind leading
Every other dance.
I like unisex in dress,
some permissive openness.
But why a zipper down the front of all my pants?

I really think the genders should be equal.
It's fun to wear a suit
With vest and tie.
But of all the gains we've made
The one I'll gladly trade
Is the embarrassment when I forget to zip my fly.

Mother Nature is a wise and caring person.
She planned that zipper
For the male anatomy.
Since women haven't changed a bit,
We still pull 'em down and sit,
Please put my zippers back where they're supposed to be.

Olga Chambers

The Little Mermaid's Awakening

For nearly two millennia, she had been waiting in the dark, the dust of untold centuries hiding the iridescent sheen of her silver scales.

As the years passed, the pain of her isolation diminished. Only fragments of memory remained: her free spirit being torn from her, the ignominy of being cast into the dark dungeon where spiders could weave their tangled cobwebs, hiding the image of her beautiful body. The mermaid's golden hair had tarnished with the mold of eternal time.

Locked away in the blackness of her underground crypt, the remainder of her captive soul screamed deep in the dead silence, but there were no ears to hear nor eyes to see her fury during those early years of her incarceration. As the years grew into eons the rage gave way to despair. Worse, by far, feelings of self-pity wreaked further destruction on her already wretched spirit. Reduced to a piteous state, the mermaid stood there, neither dead nor alive.

Only one thing remained clear in her memory. Like the reflections of a spinning crystal, Neptune's command echoed through the vacant corridors of her mind. "Never show yourselves to humans," he had thundered. "Never! For if you do, our kingdom and all that is in it shall be destroyed."

She remembered well the reasons he gave for his declaration. "Humans are an acquisitive lot. They are collectors of things; they must subdue everything in their realm. If they discover our existence, they shall possess us. By creating copies of our reality they capture our spirits." Thus, just as he predicted, it happened.

First there were glimpses and wild guesses. Then as men improved their sailing vessels, more sightings were made and the pursuit of her kind became a relentless obsession. She saw carvings of the sister mermaids she had lost riding proudly on the prows of their sailing ships, just as effigies of dragons had been set on the earliest oar-driven vessels. Had the mermaids' predecessors shed tears too? Salty tears hidden by the ocean spray?

But dragons lived before her time. She knew not their fate, though she had searched diligently as she explored the Seven Seas. She was never to see the handsome beasts except as images depicted on the prows of those heavy Nordic ships.

One by one her sisters disappeared. The images that men created stole the spirits that had once swum free. Her spirit too, as much as this mermaid had tried to conceal herself from searching eyes, was finally captured into the bronze sculpture, all that remained of the sleek and lively creature she had once been.

The artist who had created her image found himself in an unfortunate position at court, where a competitor had insinuated himself into the patron's favor. The usurper, determined not to lose his place, sent spies to see the artist's latest work. Thereupon, he caused both artist and his sculpture to disappear, never to be seen again.

The mermaid, to her horror, was walled into a crypt in the foundation of one of Germany's many castles, along with the body of her creator, whose bones had long ago turned to dust. In time, through the progression of many wars and economic changes, all that remained of the castle was a pile of rubble. The foundation had been used again and again, but progress made it necessary to remove the last remains to build a parking lot.

"Wow!" exclaimed the workman who broke through to the crypt containing the bronze mermaid. "Get a look at this!" He peered through the dust his pick had raised from opening the hollow behind the rock. A sunbeam touched the irregular green surface, revealing more as he continued to pick away. The workman's cry attracted the foreman. He walked over to see what the commotion was about. As the hole grew larger, more of the other laborers on the site formed a circle around the opening. Eager hands joined in to remove the rock as it collected at the foot of the crypt.

When they saw what it was, they were surprised. Many voices echoed the same amazement. "A mermaid! What a strange thing to find buried in a hole in the ground!" The workers milled around, each of them trying to see her. She sat on a pedestal that looked like grass and lily pads. Several fish swam around the base.

"She's supposed to be a fountain. Look at that, the fishes' mouths are open," cried one of the workmen. They stood there in admiration, for the mermaid was beautiful indeed, even through the green patina which had coated the bronze from which she had been cast.

"My friend the antique dealer in Weissensberg will be happy to sell her for us," said the owner of the property who by this time had also joined the crowd. "Then we will have a big party to celebrate, when we get done with the job." He was greeted with cheers. The workers wasted no time lifting the heavy piece out of its hiding place.

It was noon by the time Herr Schwarz arrived at the site. He backed up his pickup truck, and with the help of the workmen got the mermaid onto the flatbed. "A fine piece," Schwarz said to his friend. "I shall clean her up, and I am sure we can get a good price for her."

As Schwarz made the turn into his yard, a little blue car passed by, behind his truck.

The awakening mermaid heard voices. Betty and Wayne Cameron, with their granddaughter Heidi, were touring Germany in the rented car when they passed by Schwarz's *Antiquitaten*, with its various articles on display by the side of the country road.

Olga Chambers

The mermaid heard a child's voice cry out. "Stop!" she cried. "Gramma! Stop the car! I see a mermaid! And there's a carousel horse out there in the yard. Please stop!" Before the mermaid heard the second, "Stop!" Cameron had already stopped the car and was backing it up. By the time he pulled on the hand brake and got out of the car, his wife and granddaughter had hurried over to admire the horse.

The doors to a barn-like warehouse stood open. The mermaid saw no more, for Schwarz drove his truck inside, to the shop at the far end of the building. With a workman's help he unloaded her from the back of the truck and left her standing in the middle of the floor.

The Camerons, outside, were busy looking at the fountains, cherubs, alligators, and tortoises of assorted sizes. A Teutonic knight stood beside a three-foot-tall head of a Buddha. Sculptures of every size and shape were scattered in reckless abandon about the open field.

"Let's see what they have inside," said Betty Cameron. "That truck went in there, I'd like to find out how much they want for some of these pieces they've got out here."

"Now Betty, you need these sculptures like you need a hole in your head. Besides, how would we get something like that horse home? It's half the size of a real one." Cameron didn't need an answer. His wife was an impulse buyer, but he'd guessed the horse his granddaughter was so enamored of was undoubtedly well beyond the price they had put on the souvenirs they would be bringing back to the United States.

Inside, they found more treasures, pieces that looked like they might have come from Victorian times, others that were decidedly Art Deco, and some that might even have come from the Viking Era. Finally, they heard footsteps coming from the far end of the building. A young man, perhaps in his late thirties, came forward, addressing them in German.

"Whoa there, hold it — English," Cameron interrupted. "We only speak English." Flustered, Schwarz responded with a few words of broken English which were far more than anything the American tourists could have come up with in his language.

When queried about the price of the carousel horse, Schwarz could not make himself understood. He finally wrote a figure in Deutchemarks on a piece of paper he pulled out of his pocket, which did indeed far exceed anything they could pay for the piece.

"That's a bargain, Wayne, and if we were in the reselling market, I am sure one of those antique dealers back in Langley would give us more than twice what he's asking."

While they discussed such a possibility, Schwarz disappeared. Heidi followed her grandparents further into the building, where their footsteps sounded in hollow echoes on the oiled floorboards. She bounced from one piece to another in her excitement.

Before long, they heard Schwarz's returning footsteps. He had an attractive young woman with him. She was carrying a little boy of about 15 months. When she spoke, it was obvious that she had studied the English language, for though she spoke with an accent, her diction and syntax were excellent. "My husband welcomes you," she said. "Please feel free to look as much as you like." She went on, explaining about the markings on the pieces which showed them as being sold, marked for repair, or being sent out to other stores on consignment. She spoke hesitantly, searching for words, but she spoke well. As she moved away, Heidi followed, for her fascination with babies far exceeded any interest in inanimate objects.

The Camerons were excited over their find. Pieces from the Medieval period were in one area, and in another they found copies of Egyptian and Oriental figures in the Art Nouveau style. There was a whole section devoted to cherubs and gargoyles. It was like being in a museum, the best part of which was knowing that the pieces could be purchased. While they continued to explore, they could hear happy voices in the distance.

Heidi was making a new friend. The Camerons moved in the direction of the sounds. They found themselves in Schwarz's workshop.

"Oh, Wayne! Will you look at this!" Betty could not contain herself. She was circling around the mermaid Schwarz had left standing in the center of the floor. "Wayne, I must have her. Wouldn't she be beautiful at home, out on Deer Lake. Our very own mermaid. She is just exquisite! Is she for sale? I hope so."

"Whoa! Take it easy, Babe. Don't get so excited. You know the price goes up automatically when you do that." Heidi too, distracted from the baby and feeling her grandmother's excitement, danced around the mermaid. "I have a name for her," she cried enthusiastically. "Let's call her Birgit. You know, after the pretty waitress at the *Gast Haus* we stayed in last night." Frau Schwarz agreed that it was a good name for a mermaid who had been made by a long ago German craftsman.

With a start, the mermaid felt a quickening at Heidi's call. As surely as she had lost her soul with its own magical name when she was first captured, a new name would recover something of that lost spirit.

A name! Birgit. It had a lovely ring to it. She was Birgit! Birgit listened to the humans' talk about home and Deer Lake on Whidbey Island in the Pacific Northwest. Those names were strange. She could not guess where they were. More strongly than before, she heard the call as Heidi touched the tip of her tail. Birgit! With the magic that is childhood, the tingle of life passed from Heidi's fingers. Birgit's spirit had returned.

The Camerons settled on a price, and Schwarz indicated that he would crate the bronze appropriately for the ocean crossing. Birgit heard him say that she would be transported by rail to Hamburg, from where she would then go by cargo ship to the port nearest to Whidbey Island.

Traveling by rail? This meant no more to her than the ride had in the bed of Schwarz's pick-up truck. Had the horses gone by the way of the dragons too? The men who kidnaped her had used the beautiful beasts to cart her away. She had seen no sight of any such animals on her way to Schwarz's shop. So much was new. She could see that she had much to learn. Birgit heard Wayne Cameron telling Schwarz that he would arrange their own ground transportation once she reached the Port of Seattle.

Birgit's spirit soared. Seattle? Why did that name sound familiar? It had the sound of those ancient times when she saw children playing on the shores of a land in the northern reaches. Names she had heard long ago: Issaquah, Puyallup, Tukwilla, Snohomish. They were ancient names that dated back to the time of her own antiquity.

Heidi blew her a kiss as the family left, and she thought about being near the water again. What happiness! What joy! Very soon, she would be crated and shipped over the sea. How well she knew those distant shores. She had explored them all. But "Whidbey Island" and "Pacific" meant nothing to her, for the names men had given places must have come much after her freedom had been taken from her. Had the humans conquered all of the earth, then? Were there any survivors left of her kingdom? Surely, she thought, not all of them could have been captured.

Before long, she saw the crate being assembled in which she would be traveling. It could be a little like being in the dungeon in which she had been trapped, but that journey had an end to it. For Birgit it would be a new beginning. A new adventure.

Seattle? She searched her memory for clues to earlier times. If only she could remember. Could she be right? Her adventures exploring the edges of the lands bordering her water world had taken her to such beautiful places. The landscape was often as lovely as the sights she saw in the depths of the ocean. She had delighted in seeing icebergs which floated high above on the dark blue surface of her sea world replicated in the brilliant white clouds which gathered in pastel shades of cerulean skies overhead.

The distant canyons with their mysterious occupants were no less intriguing than the ocean's deep crevasses she had explored in the company of her companions, the whales. What she had seen under the waters was so like the mountains which crowded close to the shores. So too, were the volcanoes which spewed their rocks high into the sky like their underwater counterparts which blew huge geysers of boiling steam into the surrounding sea.

What would it be like on Deer Lake? Would she be sharing her waters with crocodiles and colorful tropical birds? Or, would there be ice and snow? She looked at the fish which surrounded her base. Would her little companions of long ago be with her again? So much to anticipate.

In Washington, Birgit's new family was also waiting. Months went by before she was put on a cargo ship destined for Seattle. Finally, the call came from the importing company's agents. Cameron borrowed a truck from a friend, and together they went to claim the shipment. By the time Heidi got home from school that day, Birgit was sitting on the lawn facing Deer Lake. Impatient as only a ten-year-old can be, Heidi wanted her Gramma to install the mermaid right away. But, as it was still winter, the lake was too cold for any work to be done in building the foundation and locating the pump.

"When the weather warms up," her grandfather said, "We will build a place out there on the lake so that she'll look like she is sitting right on the surface of the water."

Birgit had lots of practice in waiting. She knew that Heidi had much to learn about patience, but before long, the first signs of spring exploded with the show of color in the early blooming rhododendrons. Always first to blossom were the native pinks. The buds were forming that would become the hybrid yellows, the variegated peaches and the brilliant reds.

As the days warmed and the rains lessened, the lake

water level began to drop. The day finally came when Cameron woke Heidi up with the good news. "Now we build Birgit's base. Get your work clothes on."

As Birgit watched from her spot on the grass, they carefully built up the foundation to bring the base upon which she would sit, even with the high-water mark to which the lake rose in the winter. The project took several days before they could set her in place.

Heidi helped mix the cement and place the rocks around the base to conceal the cement blocks. All the while she worked, she chatted with her grandfather. Finally, they were finished. Birgit saw Heidi clap her hands as she cried, "Birgit has her own little mountain to sit on, doesn't she, Gramma?"

"That's right," Grampa replied. "We are ready to install the pump. She's ready."

"Okay, Heidi," Grampa yelled, "you can turn her on!" Heidi threw the switch and suddenly the fish on Birgit's base sang as the waters squirted from their gaping mouths.

The spray issued forth in rainbows all about her figure as the sun shone through the flying drops of water. She could feel the moisture returning the sheen to her scales. She had her name, a gift that only an innocent can bestow, love untrammeled with expectations.

Waiting till the last rays of the sun had disappeared behind the Olympics and the surface of the lake had turned to the color of burnished pewter Birgit's spirit stirred.

Behind clouds, heavy with moisture, the waxing moon broke through, leaving reflections of glittering footsteps on the water as it tiptoed closer to Birgit's quiescent figure. Like a new bride receiving her lover's embrace, she accepted the moon's kiss. The small sparkle burst to life, trembling as it grew, to reach out encompassing the stars at the far ends of the Universe. She flew with the comets and returned with the wind. She touched the tips of the mountains, and tumbled down their sides with the raindrops. She was the dew on the petals that leapt out of their buds to welcome the first rays of the sun. She flowed with the streams that ran to the oceans. Birgit's spirit was alive.

My Summer Vacation

by Gramma as Heidi Trappman

Hi. My name is Heidi. I am eleven years old, and I live with my Gramma and Grampa. We have a motorhome, a big blue and white one which we usually travel around in in the summertime. We would get to travel in it more, but I have to go to school, so that kind of stops the times we can go away.

Last summer, instead of going in the motorhome, we went to Germany. My daddy's ancestors are from Germany, and since I live with my mommy's parents, Grampa thought I should learn more about my other origins.

Grampa is organized, so we went to the library and the AAA and got a bunch of maps and travel guides. He already knew about Germany because he was in the army during World War II, but Gramma and I never saw it before. So we all read a whole bunch of stuff about it.

I like to read. Gramma says I devour books, and I

guess she's right because I read about eight paperbacks a week. I like Goosebumps, Ramona, The Babysitters Club, Nancy Drew, and the Boxcar Children. The Illustrated Classics are nice too, 'cause when I finish them we rent the movies and get to see the stories. My mommy likes to read, so my middle name is Lenore. I guess you know where that came from, and of course, everybody knows about the real Heidi. That was the first big book my Gramma read when she was little. She's just like me. She likes to read too.

I live on Whidbey Island, in Washington, so our trip started with a ferry ride. We flew on TWA from Seattle to Munich. It took us twelve hours to fly there. Gramma had reservations for a hotel on the day we landed, and that was a good thing because we were all pooped. We slept so hard the first day we missed breakfast and lunch. When we got up, it was so late we had dinner for breakfast.

Munich is a lot like Seattle. It has some nice places to see, and it has lots of museums. The big museum there was the first place we went to, and we got to see a lot of beautiful paintings. Some of them were huge. I liked the ones of the horses the best. Gramma likes to take her time, so by the time she was finished looking, she found Grampa and me on the bench in the lobby. She took a picture of us, but she didn't tell us till we got the film back from the drugstore. There I was with my head on Grampa's lap. We were both sound asleep. That was pretty funny.

The other funny thing that happened was on our way to finding the Romantiche Strasse. The tour books said that it was the road with the prettiest castles and best places to see. One of the tour books said that they named it the Romantic Highway (that's what Romantiche stands for) so that more people would come to see it. They must be right, 'cause that's what we did.

Grampa likes to take the back roads to get anywhere, because he says all the freeways do is to take you from point A to point B the fastest. So we tried to get off of the Autobahns as quickly as we could. An awful lot of the roads we passed said "Ausfahrt" on them. Gramma said we should go to Ausfahrt because it must be an important place but she couldn't find it on any of the maps. Later we figured out that it really wasn't a place at all, but just meant "Exit." Gramma felt pretty silly. When we got back after our vacation, we named our cat Ausfahrt because he has a problem and Ausfahrt is what you have to do when his problem happens. We are trying all the brands of kitten food to see if that will help, because he is a nice cat otherwise.

Anyway on the way to the Romantiche Strasse, we drove through a little town called Wurze. All the roads in town were blocked because they were having a street fair. Grampa kept trying to get through, but we had no luck. Finally he saw a big, shiny white Mercedes that looked like the people knew where they were going, so Grampa said he would follow them. We followed the car past all the entertainers' trailers that were parked along a side street behind the town hall and big, brick government buildings. We stayed right behind the other car even though it looked like he was driving straight into the fairgrounds. We were driving pretty slowly by that time because there were people all around us walking past the fancy booths all decorated with colored flags and balloons. Suddenly the driver we were following stopped next to an exhibit booth and pulled his car into a parking place right beside it. Uh-oh!

By this time Grampa decided that he was in the wrong place, but it was too late to turn around. He got awfully quiet, which is not true when he sees bad drivers that act like they don't know what they are doing. When that happens, Gramma usually shushes him when he uses the "f" words. But today he was as quiet as could be. The crowds just kept getting bigger, and he kept driving more and more slowly past the stands.

Finally we couldn't get any further. There were just

too many people, and I could hear the calliope music coming from the carousel ahead of us.

The car wasn't moving. Our windows were rolled down, and there was a man outside of my window who was yelling and was all red in the face. He was shaking his fist at us while he yelled an awful lot of things in German. I'll bet anything that he was using the "f" words too. He sure looked like he was. Everybody else was kind of staring at us, and I was so embarrassed I slid way down in my seat and covered my head with my coat. It has a hood on it, fortunately for me.

Pretty soon all the yelling attracted a couple of policemen. They started scolding us too, but they didn't get all red in the face, and when they saw we couldn't understand them, one of them talked to us in English.

They directed us to a spot where we could turn around. Everybody was standing around looking at us, and it seemed like everything at the fair had stopped except for the music. Gramma poked her camera at me and said I should get out and take a picture for the journal I was keeping. But I wasn't getting out of the car for anything. So she had to get out and take one herself.

By the time we were through turning, I think Wurze's entire police force was there. I counted seven policemen. But they were very nice to us. The policeman who could speak English even drew a map for us so that we could get out of town. His directions were funny, though. It was as if he figured we should know where we were going 'cause he told us to go past the railroad station to where the American PX used to be, figuring, I guess, that since we were Americans we should know that automatically. We didn't find the PX, but we finally did get back on the road we wanted without any more trouble.

But whenever we saw a white car after that, Gramma and I would both yell, "Don't follow the white car!"

ॐ

Murray Anderson

From Breederman

The first hard frost came the second week of November followed by a strong northeast wind coming out of Canada. Even with the protection of the surrounding woods from the cold wind, the morning required an extra coat and another pair of wool socks in my boots, and the milkings always started out cold until the heat of the cows warmed the barn. After milking, the cows loitered in the doorway of the barn while I had to yell and shove them out into the cold before closing the door.

Each morning I welcomed the warmth of the kitchen and breakfast. I dreaded returning to the outside where knuckles bruised, hands chapped, feet numbed; all of this, combined with clumsy clothes and gloves, made the work harder.

That Friday we heard a pickup come into the yard. "Sounds like Fronson," Carol said as she parted the curtains. "It's him, all right. I wonder what he wants? Do you know?"

"Last time he left mad. Haven't heard from him since. Not a peep." I put another hotcake on my plate and reached for the syrup.

Footsteps moved across the porch, then there was a rap on the door. "Coming," Carol said. She opened the door. "Why, Mr. Fronson, come in." She motioned him to the chair closest to the stove.

"It's cold out there." He rubbed his hands together and took off his heavy fleece-lined jacket.

"Here, give me that," Carol said.

"That's okay." He shrugged her away and put it on the back of his chair.

"Coffee?" Carol said.

"Yeah, that would be good." He sat down in the chair. "How the cows doing?"

"A little better now with so many fresh. But this cold snap won't help," I said.

"It's good weather to kill and butcher." He leaned forward. "This cold got me to thinking. You have any cows we should cull?"

"There's old Bullhead. Still haven't got her bred, and she's almost dry."

"Well, we're about out of meat in the freezer, and I was wondering if we could make a deal. You do the butchering for a half? That's the way Cavesal and I had it worked out. Although sometimes I think he cheated, taking more than he should."

"Yeah, I wouldn't doubt it," I said and wondered whether he had kept any better track of this than he did with his other dealings with Cavesal.

"You provide the wrapping paper and the knives and such?" I asked, cutting my hotcake and taking a bite.

"I have the knives and saws that I had before I moved off the farm you can use, but the paper — I don't know. Can't you use newspapers?"

"No, freezes on the meat," Carol said, filling our cups. "It's real messy and the meat's hard to thaw and clean up."

"Oh hell, buy some butcher paper on my account at Midvalley Meats. Get a small roll. While you're picking that up, why don't you drop by my place and get the knives."

Paddy Bloomquist brought his gun and some of his knives. His specialty in the neighborhood was butchering, in exchange for a roast or some liver or a steak or two.

Short, stocky Paddy had married large-boned, pleasant Tootie after the first year of college, saying he was lonesome for the farm and Tootie. According to Paddy, Tootie had threatened to drop him if he didn't come home. Tootie's old man, Roy Larson, was alive then, and Paddy, when he was growing up, worked every summer for Roy.

As Paddy said, he and Larson had a good understanding, got along as well as a young fiery Irishman and a stubborn Norwegian widower could under the circumstances. He and Tootie were another thing, not paying much attention to each other until the summer before he left for college when "we got a little thicker in the haymow," as Tootie put it. Then the Second World War started, and Larson offered a partnership and Paddy received a deferment to stay on the farm. When the old man died after the war, Tootie and Paddy took over the farm.

Out of sight of the road, in the pasture beside the barn, Paddy'd set out a bale of straw and unrolled an old bed sheet where he laid out knives, sharpener, meat cleaver and saw. Bullhead, left alone in the stanchion, bellered to the empty barn and the cows outside. She jerked back, banging the metal stanchion, creating a clatter that rocked the inside of the barn.

"I'll get my gun," Paddy said as I headed toward the machine shed to get the tractor. He pulled his twenty-two from behind the seat of the pickup and grabbed a box of shells from the glove compartment.

"It's a good day for killing," Paddy said as he waddled in his boots through the frost-covered grass toward the bale and his knives. "The meat will be cold, easy to handle, no flies." He laid the gun down on the bale and picked up the stained apron. "Where you going to kill her?" he said as I started the tractor.

"In the holding pen over there." I pointed to the back of the barn. He followed me, walking in the hard frozen ruts. The cows — alert, sharp-eyed, and worried — lined up along the fence to follow our progress.

"How the hell do they know what we're going to do?" I yelled at Paddy over the noise of the tractor.

"Always happens. Never fails," Paddy answered, shaking his head, shifting the twenty-two to his other hand. "Beats all, doesn't it?"

I jumped off the tractor and went into the barn. Bullhead turned and watched me open the bottom half of the door. Her frightened eyes followed me as I went in front of her and filled the feed scoop with grain. Thinking that I was going to let her out, she jerked back, rattling her stanchion again. I poured the grain on a clean spot near the corner of the holding pen where Paddy could get a good shot at her when she came out.

I opened her stanchion. She backed out, slipped on the slick manure, lost her footing, got up, ran into the yard, circled, and brushed against the fence until she came to the grain. She lowered her head, smelled the grain. Just as Paddy cocked the gun, she lifted her head, snorted, and paced around the pen again, looking for an escape until she came to the grain. Paddy leaned on the fence, finger of his ungloved hand on the trigger.

"Thunk!" The twenty-two barked, and Bullhead, amazed, staggered back, crumpled, and rolled on her side. I opened the gate for Paddy. He rushed by me, pulling out his knife from the scabbard on his belt as he ran to the shaking brindle body. He pulled her head back and slashed across her neck. As blood spurted out, he reached down with his other hand and cleaned away the opening so the blood ran freely.

"Well that's over. Let her bleed for a while," Paddy said, reaching under his apron for a cigarette. We turned our backs, and while he cupped his hand over the cigarette, we looked out over the woods through the leafless tree to the frost-covered pastures down on the river bottom below.

"Cavesal would be happy now. She's dead. He beat her," I said. "I caught him doing it. The way the other cows act, I don't think she was the only one."

"He sure hated cows," Paddy said as he took a drag on his cigarette, removed it from his mouth, looked at the glowing tip. "Can't understand him staying with dairying, milking cows." He shook his head and tossed the cigarette into the blood, where it sizzled and died. "Well, I suppose we'd better string her up."

The cows outside the pen circled, sniffed for the scent of the blood. The wild-eyed ones, like trotters, paced along the fence and snorted white smoke into the October air.

"Better get her out of here quickly so they can settle down," Paddy said.

In the orchard away from the barn we skinned and gutted the cow. It took all day to cut and pack the meat. Carol's experience butchering moose and bear in Alaska was soon evident as she took to the task. Sara came over to help keep the two babies quiet and content. The clock over the sink said four when we wrapped and marked the last package; it was milking time. I washed off at the kitchen sink and changed clothes to get rid of the blood spots that had soaked through the apron that was smeared with grease and blood. The grease stuck to my hands though I washed them thoroughly.

Grabbing three cookies by their edge, I left the cleanup and dividing with Carol and Sara and went to the milkhouse. When I drove the cows through the barn door, they shied away from the blood on the concrete in the yard.

I saw Fronson's pickup backed up to the porch. He leaned over the bed and counted packages of meat as he put them in boxes in back of his pickup. He never came to the barn any more when I was milking, especially if he was wearing his going-to-town cowboy shirt and whipcord pants.

A week before Thanksgiving Ma called while I was still in the barn. "How are you, Jack? And how's your little princess?" she asked. "When you coming to visit again? I haven't seen you."

"We've been busy, Ma, like I told you over the phone last week," I said. I heard the click of Carol hanging up the house phone.

"You still there, Jack? I thought we'd been disconnected," Ma said.

"No, I'm here in the barn just finishing up," I said, checking my watch. "Getting ready to go in and eat."

"It's November already. Time sure flies," she said and then was quiet for a while. "I've been lonesome. When am I going to see you?"

"I know, Ma. Like I said, we've been busy."

"So busy you couldn't visit your mother who is all alone. Jack, I thought I raised you to be more thoughtful than that," she said, clucking.

"Hey, Ma I just remembered Carol wants me to ask if you would have Thanksgiving with us. How about that?"

"We'll I don't know," she said. "I can't drive. Could you come get me?"

"Sure Ma, I'll get you."

"If Carol needs some help, I can come on Wednesday and cook or take care of the baby," she said.

"Sure, Ma. I'll see what Carol wants to do."

"See what Carol wants to do?" she sighed. "Oh, I suppose that's right, but let me know."

The warm lights of the house fell on the packed earth path and beckoned through the crisp evening air as I walked toward the house. On the porch I scuffed off my boots and hung up my coat. The trash burner in the kitchen, along with the wood stove crackling in the living room, cloaked the house with warmth that went clear to the heart. I relished this time of night. Tired but satisfied with the day's achievement, welcomed by the women folded about my life, I wondered if other men coming home from work enjoyed it as much as I did.

"Hi, Honey. How'd milking go?" Carol asked.

"Pretty good, actually."

"Was that your mother on the phone? Did you ask her about Thanksgiving?"

"She wants to come Wednesday," I said as I picked up Leona who'd crawled to my chair.

"Yes?" Carol said, waiting for my response. "Well?"

"I said I'd go get her and she could be with us. She doesn't have anyone up there."

"What else? What else did she say?"

"Not much, just that she'd help with the cooking and taking care of Leona. That's all." I lifted Leona up and blew on her bare stomach to her wiggling and giggling.

"What did you say?"

"I said I'd talk to you about it." I pulled down Leona's dress and set her on the floor. "I said I'd let her know."

"Well I don't know. I really don't need help to get ready. I have things under control." Carol went to the stove and stirred the stew pot. "It's not that I don't like her. It's that she just takes over, and this is my house and I think I can handle it."

"You forget it's my house too," I said picking up Leona and putting her in her high chair. "It's only one day."

"I know it is. I'm sorry. We're arguing again." She came around the table with a bowl of stew and set it in front of me. She brushed back my hair and kissed me on my forehead as the smell of the stew mixed with the remnants of the perfume she wore. "That Wednesday is our fourth anniversary. Maybe we can have Ma baby-sit and we can go out. It's been nine months since Leona was born, and we haven't been alone anywhere."

"Why don't you call Ma and ask her?" I put down my fork and moved my arms around her waist and squeezed her to me. "I think that'd be nice."

That Wednesday evening, Carol came from the bedroom wearing the dress I saw on our first coke date. She twirled around in front of Ma and me. "It still fits. How do you like it?"

"Great. Takes me back a few years," I said noticing the way she'd bobbed her hair and how tanned she looked even this late in the year. Tonight the hard work didn't show, only youthful exuberance. Ma surveyed her daughter-in-law with a slight smile and taking Leona's hand pointed toward Carol. Leona's wide eyes followed her mother around the room.

This was a small pleasure for Carol, something that transcended the tough days, the hard work, and the birth and care of a baby. To think she could have married someone else, lived in a house with a furnace, carpets on the floor, new overstuffed furniture, and a real car, not a beat up pickup filled with grain sacks, tool chests, shovels, and forks. I wondered if she ever thought of things like that when she looked at the snapshots of her college days.

We left Ma with the girls and drove to a dinner of hamburgers and fries taken through the window at the A&W while the pickup ran to keep us warm and "My Foolish Heart" came over the radio. I raised my chocolate malt. "Happy anniversary!" I said. "Welcome to the greasy chef's delight. I told you you could have done better, but you wouldn't listen. You should've known things would be like this after that honeymoon at the Mountain View Motel."

She picked up her milkshake and touched mine. "Happy fourth anniversary to the best husband a girl could deserve."

The parking lot was almost full at the Grange Hall. Listening to the polka and the shouts and laughs coming from the hall, we dashed over the frozen ground to the entryway. Inside, the warm air took away the chill as I handed our coats to the woman in the cloak room and bought tickets. Then we had our hands stamped and went through the double doors to the dance floor. A new band, the Western Ramblers, was playing the "Beer Barrel Polka."

"There's Sara and John," Carol said. She led me across to the other side of the dance floor where they were standing next to the Christmas tree.

Carol and Sara hugged and laughed while John and I shook hands. The women moved away, chattering about their babies. John, the muscles of his long arms filling his sweater, leaned his lanky body against the wall. Though shy in a crowd, he moved with the confidence good health brings.

It was just after we'd moved in that I had coffee with him at the sales barn. He told me about his first milking job for a neighbor near Sunshine, Iowa, after he and Sara were married and he quit school. This was his third farm. He and Sara had moved from Iowa last fall just before Christmas, answering an ad in the *Northwest Farmer*. With so little education, he was destined to this hard work like so many milkers I'd known. Even if they enjoyed working with cows, they'd finally tire of the early and long days, little time off,

Murray Anderson

and the hard work. Then they'd get a job with the county or
city road crew, a sawmill upriver, or a feed store packing
sacks around.

John cleared his throat. "Lost one of our best cows," he
said. "Had some trouble calving, retained her afterbirth.
Doc Erlandson come out and cleaned her, but she didn't do
well, wouldn't eat, ran a fever. He couldn't figure it out. We
filled her with penicillin shots and sulfa pills and tried some
other new-fangled antibiotic. Don't remember its name, but
she just got worse, lost weight, nothing but skin and bones."
He shifted to his other foot and changed hands against the
wall.

"One day I comes out to milk and finds her dead in the
box stall. I calls Erlandson and tells him. He comes right
out. Said he wanted to do a postmortem. So we gets in his
pickup and we follows Dimmick in his dead animal truck to
the rendering plant, and after they get her dumped on the
ground, Doc slits her open and the pus runs out of her
uterus like tomato soup. She was just full of peritonitis.
Erlandson stood there, doesn't say nothin', just shakes his
head. He should've known to treat her uterus now that I
look back, but hell, those things happen. At the time, I
didn't know either, but he's the vet. Well, heck — you win
some, you lose some." He shook his head. "The boss wasn't
too happy about that one. Harley's so tight, I think he might
refuse to pay Erlandson — at least make him wait for a
while. How's things going with you?"

"Still struggling along. You know how it is this time of
year. Everything seems hard."

"Someday I'd just like to up and leave Old Harley
Johnson, the cheapskate, and find me a better job. One
where I had some time off. He gives me a day off every
other week. You'd think he was giving me a trip to Hawaii
every time I say it's my weekend off. He fumes and fusses
like a steer in a pen full of heifers in heat. Hell, we'd like to
go to see Sara's folks oftener, especially with the baby here.
But we just can't get away. If you hear of anything at those
dairy meetings, you could let me know. I wouldn't mind

moving to Skagit County either." He changed hands against the wall and jacked one foot up on the edge of the wooden bench.

"You tried this artificial bull stud yet?" he said. "Old Johnson won't hear it, says it costs too much." He straightened up and looked around the room, not lifting his eyes too high. He ran his hands through his sandy crewcut. "That sneaky son-of-a-bitch of a bull we got now scares the shit out of me. I don't trust him farther than you can throw a horse. He's been tearing his pen up, tossing three-by-eights and ten-foot fence posts around. I'm afraid he's going to get out. I know there should be two of us around when I go in to clean his pen, but Harley's always too busy or gone to town when I need him to help. Just finds excuses and leaves it up to me. I keep telling him he'd better have his insurance paid up."

"He's sure loud — the bull, I mean," I said. "I can hear him bellering like hell every time you breed a cow."

A feedback screech came over the loudspeakers, and a blond stocky band member announced, "Next we'll have a schottische for you Norwegians." And the thump-a-thump-a-thump began again. Carol broke away from Sara and grabbed my hand. "Can't you guys talk about anything but cows?"

"Heck, what would you want us to do, talk about our old girlfriends?" I said as we went to the middle of the floor, then hopped and swung off into the crowd.

"It's nice to see Sara and John getting out," Carol said when the band had stopped and we were walking back to them.

The announcer bent over the microphone, tapped, and blew into it. "I guess this thing's on. How'd you like that one?" he said, bringing applause, whistles, and hoots from the crowd. Clearing his throat again he said, "We have a request for 'My Foolish Heart' for Jack and Carol Swenson, who are celebrating their fourth anniversary. Let's give them a hand."

With John and Sara grinning and pushing us we walked

out onto the middle of the floor to applause. I held Carol close — my head in her scented hair, my arms around her waist — and as the other couples closed in around us, we were back at the spring dance at college even though the weather was November.

After the dance, we stopped at the A&W again and had milkshakes and listened to the music on the radio.

"Let's go down by the river and park." Carol laid her head on my shoulder and ran her hand down my thigh.

"What time is it?"

She twisted away and squinted at her watch, using the lights from the neon sign to see. "Almost eleven. Let's go. It's on the way home."

"It's late, but oh heck, I can take a nap tomorrow." I shifted into reverse and backed away and swung out onto the almost deserted streets of Arlington. I turned off the main highway and followed the River Road, bumping out onto an open space overlooking the Stillguamish River. With so much of the rain falling as snow in the mountains and foothills, the river was low, and reflections of the moon and stars played along the water bouncing over the riffles. Since it was November, no one else was making out in parked cars. Leaving the car running and the heater on full and the radio playing "Slow Boat to China," we kissed slowly and passionately.

"Oh, damn, I forgot. No diaphragm!" Carol pushed me away and straightened up. She started counting on her fingers. "Lets see. This is the 28th, right? I think I'm okay." Then she lifted her skirt and struggled until she victoriously flung her panties on the dashboard. I twisted from under the steering wheel, bumping the gearshift into reverse and killing the motor. Carol giggled and threw her leg up behind me. And I fell on her, bumping my knee on the gearshift again. The music faded into the background as I slipped my hands under her bra, grasping her breasts, breathing heavily, having as much trouble making connections as switching a gearshift on a long- haul truck.

Lying there on top of Carol, I heard the music drift back

into my consciousness. "Happy anniversary, Honey," I said. The music stopped, and the twelve o'clock news came on with a weather forecast of snow and colder temperature.

"Lucky you didn't have a car when we were going to school or this would not be our fifth anniversary," she said.

I was hardly in bed when the alarm rang, and in a fog I made it to the barn and moved slowly through the milking. I cleaned the barn and the milkhouse and fed silage to the cows, then crossed the yard in the rain to the house to be met by the smell of turkey in the oven. It was nice to have Ma home with us and to have someone to keep Leona occupied while Carol prepared Thanksgiving dinner. After dinner I took a quick nap, and soon Carol was shaking me. "It's three," she said. "Time to take Ma home."

Two days later the first flakes of snow slashed through the beam of the yard light as I left the house. The wind, out of the northeast, had picked up. I zipped my army pile jacket tight to my chin and pulled an olive drab knit cap down over my ears. The cold was getting serious. The temperature had dropped twenty degrees since last night. The ice in the mud puddles in the driveway had gradually settled, sloping down from the sides to the middle. Through the darkness, the milkhouse lights shone on the walkway. When I opened the door, the heater thermostat clicked on as the cold air followed me in. I closed the door quickly and turned on the faucet, left dripping last night to keep it from freezing. After a slow start, the drip grew into a steady stream. While the hot water ran, I measured out a teaspoon of powdered chlorine into the rinsing bucket for disinfecting the teat cups and then another into the bucket that I used for washing the udders.

During winter cold spells my hands would crack from chlorine and cold, and hurt at night when I was trying to sleep. The pain would also be there if a wrench slipped off a bolt and I banged my knuckles or if I didn't put on gloves when I handled coarse alfalfa bales. I wheeled the wash cart with the steaming buckets to the barn. The cows were waiting at the door. I jumped to the side as the herd rushed by me in from the cold. Praise and Jewellette's stalls were empty. They were usually the first in the barn.

From the shelf by the door I grabbed a flashlight. I checked the loafing shed. Only a few dry cows turned toward me, then went back to sleep. There it was. Damn, I'd forgotten to close the gate to the winter pasture before I left for the barn last night. With the lights of the barn behind me and the flashlight picking up shadows, I stumbled on the frozen ground toward the wood lot where the cattle liked to bed down during warmer nights. I swung my flashlight in a 180-degree arc and caught the reflection of two glowing eyes following my progress. In the flashlight beam I saw the cows, their winter coats sprinkled with snow. One was standing, one lying down. Skiffs of snow circled the ice on the puddles that had not drained off before the cold set in. I lengthened my stride to cover the ground, yelling "Ca Boss! Ca Boss!"

Jewellette, her back hunched, faced away from the wind. She looked out onto the ice where Praise sprawled, stomach flat against the ground, head laid to the side and rear legs spread like a frog swimming in a pond. I'd seen cattle in this position. I knew her pelvis was broken. I worked my way across the ice to her. In her efforts to get up, she had broken through and now lay on the crushed ice in six inches of water, dead.

Born within days of each other, Praise and Jewellette had shared neighboring calf pens for the first six months. On summer evenings after milking when I visited the yearling heifers in their hill pasture they were always together. If I petted one the other would be there to share the attention. After they had freshened with their first calves, I gave them stanchions next to each other. In the lane coming from the field they were together. In the pecking order of the herd they were equal.

Now Jewellette wouldn't budge. I pushed on her, and she moved around the edge of the pond, but she wouldn't leave. I slapped her on the back and yelled. Finally she turned and headed toward the barn. She stopped, looked back, gave a soft moo, waited for a response, then continued on. Walking into bitter northeast wind I thought of Praise and the nice calf that she had in the barn and her mother Pearlette, daughter of Pearl, who was the daughter of Quality Farms Lollipops Colleen, our first registered animal on the farm. Now Praise, an eager, easy keeper with such a future, just in her prime, gone, our herd diminished by one — not just a number but one of the best. Like so much of farming: you go ahead two and fall back one, maybe two. You get used to it. Cows die. Calves are born. But some losses hurt more than others.

At the barn, Jewellette went into her stall next to the empty one.

"You're late," Carol said as I slipped off my boots and rubbed my cold feet. "What's the matter? You look like you've seen a ghost or lost a friend." She put a plate on the table.

"I did," I said, holding my head in my hands, hiding tears. "I did. I lost a friend."

"What do you mean?"

"Praise." I said. "She's dead."

"Oh no!" Carol came to my side and laid her hands on my shoulder. "How? What happened?"

"Slipped on the ice in one of those ponds by the woods. Cows aren't made to walk on ice. Cracked her pelvis. Froze to death." I walked to the sink to wash my hands. "Damn, if I'd remembered to close that gate or if ... just a little sooner. But she was already cold."

"It's not your fault. You couldn't drain all the puddles. Or know they'd go out to the night pasture." She walked back to the stove.

"But the hard part was Jewellette," I said. "You know how they were always together. She wouldn't leave her. I had to drive her away." I shook my head as I wiped my hands on the dish towel.

"Here, Honey, eat. That might help." Carol scraped the eggs and ham from the frying pan onto my plate.

Murray Anderson 135

From the back bedroom, we heard Leona cry. "Somebody else wants breakfast," she said, putting the fry pan on the back of the stove. "You'll have to get your own coffee. Toast is about ready."

She came back with Leona and placed her in the high chair. Leona closed her arms around her teddy bear while Carol put on Leona's bib and poured warm water into the Pablum, stirring, blowing, testing with her tongue. "That's just right," she said as she filled the spoon.

"Could you call Dimmick, the dead animal man?" I said after breakfast. "I got to get right out to chores. You know, you'd think a man could cry more over something like this. Dad used to ask me when he heard about a cow tragedy or I told him bad news: He'd say, 'Did anybody in the family die? Are the kids still healthy?' And he was right."

The week before Christmas, with breakfast out of the way, Carol, who'd been quiet through the meal, put the last of the dishes in the sink. then ran water over them. Leona was making pies with her oatmeal. The stove crackled. I stretched and took a sip of my coffee.

"Damn, I wish it would warm up. This can't go on forever, but there's always more of the same."

"Do you want to hear another forecast?" Carol said, turning around and leaning on the drain board. "I don't know if it's good or bad."

"Well, you got me guessing."

"You shouldn't have to guess, just remember our anniversary. I've missed my period. I think Leona may have a brother on the way."

"Oh, my god! By the river? In the pickup?"

"Yes, in that romantic spot."

I got up and kissed her, held her close, then stepped back as I watched tears form and fill her eyes with half a sparkle.

"Uh-oh!" I said. "How do you feel about that?" She turned to the sink and picked up the dishrag, then stopped the dishrag halfway into a drinking glass.

"I don't know. Happy, I guess, happy that Leona won't be raised alone like you and I were; but I was hoping we could wait a couple years until we are on our own farm and more on our feet. Money is so tight. But what about you?" she said, dropping the unwashed glass and dishrag and turning toward me. "Are you happy?"

"I'm happy, too." I turned her toward me, kissed her, then hugged her as I looked over her shoulder, through the window where the bright sun cleared the Cascades. "Now I might have a son to work a farm with." I stood back from her as I held her hands. "And Leona will have a brother or sister to play with, to fight with, to grow up with. I don't know how many nights I dreamed of having a brother or sister. It was so lonely. Maybe I wouldn't have such a problem with Ma there'd been someone else for her to focus on, not just me."

"But Jack, can we afford another baby?"

"There's not much choice. But we'll make out."

On the Friday before Christmas, I went to the old farm to pick Ma up so she could spend Christmas weekend with us. Even though it was almost noon when I drove into the yard at the home place, Christmas tree lights shone through the living room window. Barney came out of the barn where he had bedded down with the heifers during the day to keep warm. He shuffled along on his arthritic legs, slowly wagging his tail, and caught up with me before I reached the house. Ma had been watching from the window. She met us at the door and held it open for Barney, while he cautiously and painfully made it up the three steps onto the porch.

"Hi, Ma," I said as I waited for him. "This cold weather isn't helping Barney very much."

"He's just getting old like me. This cold, when will it stop? And we aren't in the really bad part of winter yet."

"Yeah, and we'll probably run out of feed before there's any pasture."

The stove in the living room flooded the house with wood-fire warmth. While Ma poured coffee, I went into the living room and backed up to the warm stove. Barney settled on the floor by my feet.

"You're letting Barney in the house now?" I said, reaching down and ruffling his fur. He he turned and licked my hand.

"He stays in at night." Ma raised her voice in the kitchen. "It got so cold on the porch that I couldn't see leaving him outside. Besides, he's company now that he's settled down in his old age. We get along good, just the two of us. But sometimes we both get lonesome. Coffee's ready." She held out the chair at Dad's place and I sat down. "Do you want a bite to eat before we go?" She moved toward the stove, and the cast iron pan bubbled out the smell of a soup. "I got some 'stoop' here." Stoop, half way between stew and soup was what Ma made for cold days.

"Sure," I said. "It's a long ride and I haven't had lunch." I shook the milk pitcher, mixing the fat with the milk, then poured it into my glass. "Didn't I smell fresh baked bread when I came in?"

"Fresh bread is hard to hide and hard to keep when it's found," she said as she picked up hot pad holders and opened the oven. "I think these are done." She poked the top of the bread and looked along the sides of the pan. "Yes, they're done."

While I ate, she asked how Leona was doing. How was she growing? How many teeth did she have? Was she talking? Then she said, "How's things going with you and Carol?"

"Fine, fine," I said, stroking a slab of butter onto the still warm bread. "She's happy, but sometimes lonesome for her folks. Why'd you ask?"

"Oh, since this is her first real winter on the farm, I just wondered. You know it can get you down."

"But Ma, she's used to long cold winters in Alaska, so this is like early spring to her."

"Yes, I suppose it is."

"I guess you heard we lost Praise. Fell on the ice, broke her pelvis."

"That's awful. 'That's farming,' as Sig would say." She picked up the stoop pot and spoon, motioning to my bowl.

"You want some more?"

"No, no. I'm full, Ma," I said, patting my stomach.

"Well, you should have some pie before we leave," she said as she set down the pot, and then as an afterthought. "How's Carol, healthwise?"

"Carol's fine, fine," I said, "Why you asking? She's fine."

"I was just wondering when she was going to get pregnant again. You aren't going to stop with one, are you? You need a boy to balance the family out and help you with the farm."

"Well, I... as a matter of fact, she is pregnant. At least we think so."

"How wonderful! Another grandchild. How does she feel about that?"

"She likes it, I think," I said as I shifted in my chair and reached down to pet Barney, who had placed himself against my leg.

"Maybe she'll need my help this time around," Ma said as she turned to the cardboard box she'd placed on the drainboard when I first came in. "I made some pies for Christmas," she said, pointing to the box. "I hope that won't be a bother to Carol. There's some other things, too."

"Ma, Carol will be delighted, you know that," I said, drinking the last coffee in my cup. "Is that your suitcase there by the door? Is it ready to go?" I got up as Barney scrambled to stay clear of my feet.

I started the pickup to warm it up and loaded Ma's stuff while she closed down the dampers on the stove and made sure all the faucets dripped a little. So far nothing had frozen up in the house, but this was a different kind of winter. The last thing she did was turn off the Christmas tree lights.

Barney followed us to the end of the driveway, then turned and sulked back toward the barn.

"I don't like to leave Barney out in the cold ," Ma said as she looked back at him. "Maybe he would be happier at your place. There's not much to keep him interested."

"He'll go to the barn and cuddle up to the heifers. He's carrying a good coat on his back. He'll be all right. Barney's good company. You need to keep him here."

I carried Ma's suitcase and she carried the box of food up on the porch. Carol opened the door and we were met by the smell of baking turkey.

"Here, Ma, I'll take that." And before Ma could object, Carol relieved her of the box while Leona hung onto Carol's skirt sucking her thumb, looking up at Ma.

"How's my baby?" Ma advanced toward Leona. "Want to come to Grandma?" Leona turned away and hid behind Carol as Ma circled around Carol. "Come on, don't be afraid. Grandma won't hurt you."

"She's just shy," Carol said as she put the box on the drainboard and Ma retreated to a chair at the table.

"She doesn't know me. I don't get to see her often enough for her to get used to me," Ma said.

The chores went well, and as I crossed the yard toward the house, the lights of the Christmas tree shone through the window and sent colors dancing onto the porch, the trees in the orchard, and the night beyond. I stopped and peered through the window. Carol had heard me on the porch and got up to baste the turkey while Ma counted little pigs on Leona's toes. The window steamed from the heat inside and gave a soft fuzzy glow to the scene.

Dinner plates surrounded a table filled with mashed potatoes and gravy and candied sweet potatoes, while biscuits were stacked under a dishtowel. It was true that no matter how poor you were, no one starved on a farm. On the other end of the table was a plate of neat wedges of lefsa that Ma had made.

Lefsa, an old-country Christmas tradition, had been passed from generation to generation. With a flour-covered rolling pin Ma rolled out the boiled potato and flour mixture into large sheets on the kitchen table, then placed the thin, long spatula that Dad had carved from cedar under the sheet and skillfully flipped it onto the flour-sprinkled top of the woodstove. When the lefsa was baked, she'd use the lefsa stick to remove it from the stove. She covered it with melted butter, cinnamon and brown sugar, and rolled or cut it into pie-shaped slices.

Another old-country custom was the special Christmas feeding of the stock. Dad saved the best of the hay for Christmas Eve and instructed me to fill the feed scoop full when I fed the cows. Somehow, even with the rush to the house to the Christmas tree and the presents, I felt a sense of satisfaction when I closed the door on the cattle in a warm barn. My Christmas treat for the cattle would have disappointed Dad this year, but with the cold weather and the dwindling supply of good hay, I was holding back the hay for sick cows.

"Which way we going? Right or left?" I said, holding the plate of potatoes.

"It's always left," Ma said. "Have you forgot what I taught you?"

We all dug in while Leona banged her spoon on her highchair. After the first bite, Ma said, "When's the baby due, Carol?"

There was an awkward pause as Carol looked at me with surprise. I sawed away at my turkey and avoided her eyes.

"Baby? Who told you?" Carol dropped her fork on her plate.

"Jack said he thought you were pregnant. Isn't that true?"

"It could be. I'm not sure. I have to go to the doctor. We may be jumping the gun." Carol glared at me.

The cold persisted. Each morning in my patched Korean War parka, long underwear, double wool socks, bib overalls and cumbersome gloves, I thawed pipes and pried and chipped silage loose from the sides of the silo. With an ax from the woodshed, I hacked through the ice on the watering trough and pitched the ice blocks over the edge, sliding them across the concrete like hockey pucks, while thirsty cows milled around, butting their way to the trough to drink.

The cows ate more and produced less. Balky tractors and pickups refused to start. Cow pies froze to the concrete and accumulated like checkers on a playing board. If I asked for help to freeze-proof the house or barn or milkhouse, Fronson forgot about it immediately, and I was forced to make do with what I had. He knew the weather would change and I'd forget before the next freeze. But it was the winter of 1954. Soon the haymow developed open areas. All close sources of hay resupply ran out, and the farmers and feed dealers looked to California. At the Burlington siding, boxcars were unloaded of a cargo as valuable as gold.

The county extension agent on KSNO suggested rolled oats might be more economical than hay. I bought rolled oats from Hansen's Feed and spread it over the top of the silage, but the demand caused the price of rolled oats to go up, making it too expensive to feed. Farmers turned to rain-spoiled hay that for years had taken up space in the back of their haymows or some shed. They pulled it out and put it in feed racks so hungry cows could fill their empty stomachs with the brown musty stuff. Milk prices edged up because of lower production, but not enough to make up the difference in the cost of feed.

Some farmers sold out, but there weren't many buyers; only the well-heeled got good buys and expanded their herds and acreage. The bottom cows in the herd were sent to the slaughterhouse, and beef prices dropped. Heifers and young stock ate what was left and soon became lethargic and slab-sided, stunted for life. And we waited for spring.

Ann Adams.

The Secret Life of Paula Twitty

"*Tosca, finalmente mia!*" The evil Scarpia loomed over her, his face a tapestry of broken commandments, and Tosca saw her own degradation in his drooling mouth and wormy eyes. If he touched her, it would be her doom, for nothing but death could erase defilement by his horny hands.

The passionate black-eyed beauty, the toast of Rome, Tosca drew back her coal-black mane and plunged the letter-opener into his evil heart, and the blood rushed out with his raspy cries of *"Maledetta!"*

"This is Tosca's kiss!" she sang, and as he staggered toward her, she pushed him away and shrank back, shuddering.

He begged her for help *("Aiuto! aiuto!")* as the music crashed, and she taunted him: "Killed by a woman!" As he struggled for his last breath, she sang, "Does your blood choke you? *Muori! Muori! Muori!* (Die! Die! Die!)" When he lay still, she bent over him. *"E morto.* Now I forgive him."

"*Brava! Brava!*" The audience rose as one person and cheered till they grew hoarse. There were whistles and the stamping of feet, and as she bowed humbly, a strand of her coal-black hair fell over one golden shoulder. Baskets of flowers from her worshipers were crowding the other performers off the stage, but the flowers she held in her arms, a cascade of camellias, were from her lover, Placido Domingo, who was standing in the front row with his arms held out to her and tears running down his face. Outside the Rome opera house, police were holding back the crowds and the early editions of the papers were already on the streets proclaiming, "All Rome trembles before American soprano Paula Twitty, the voice of the century."

"Watch where you're going!" a raspy voice said in her ear. The sidewalk in front of the travel agent's window was crowded, and Paula had bumped Crazy Louie with her grocery cart, which held everything she owned in the world. She slapped his horny hand as it closed over a good tomato she had found in a garbage can. He gave her an evil look from a face that was a tapestry of broken commandments, and she shrank back and let him take it. Someday she would get him for all the things he stole from her, but now she sought to stop her tears by turning her gaze back to the pictures of the Rome opera house and the Palazzo Farnese.

"Never mind, darling." Elizabeth the Swede put her motherly arms around Paula, and Louie shuffled off. He wouldn't want to get into another fist fight with Elizabeth after the way she beat him up the last time. He still explained to anybody who would listen that he almost had her when his foot slipped, but whenever he found himself in her vicinity, he remembered that he had urgent business elsewhere.

"How good of you to come to my little party," the Queen said, turning her back on her other guests and drawing Paula into a corner. "Your book has not only made clear that the historical wrongs done to women are the direct cause of the mess we are in, but it has moved world leaders to act."

"Elizabeth." Paula blushed modestly and bowed her head. She would not insult this enlightened woman by calling her "Your Majesty."

The Secretary General of the United Nations approached with an expectant smile on his face, but the Queen frowned at him and he moved away, crestfallen. "He can meet you later," the Queen said to Paula, "but we have so little time together, and I want to ask your advice about the most graceful way to abolish the monarchy."

For the next hour, Paula chatted with the Queen, who didn't miss a beat when she had to turn refusing eyes on the

144   *Beneath the Rain Shadow*

world dignitaries who tried to approach them. They talked about everything from how to deal with rebellious teenage children to the best way to stop continental drift. In between, they traded some recipes. At last the Queen's eyes, as they glanced past Paula, grew warm and she said, "But I can't keep you any longer."

"Your Majesty." A distinguished looking gray-haired man bent over the Queen's hand.

"Welcome to the British Embassy," the Queen said. "My dear, may I present Dr. Stanislaus Jumbletsky, the chairman of the selection committee. I fear that he has come to take you away."

The auditorium was crowded with all the living writers Paula had ever heard of. Saul Bellow was beaming at John Updike, who looked back at him from a long, grave face. Norman Mailer was cringing before Susan Brownmiller. Milan Kundera was chatting with Italo Calvino — in Italian, Paula wondered, or Czech? She was not close enough to hear. Toni Morrison was explaining something to Anne Tyler, while Tom Wolfe listened and took notes. As Dr. Jumbletsky led her down the aisle, a hush fell over the room. On the stage he kept her hand as he said into the microphone, "My friends, I have here with me today the person who has done more for the human race than any woman since Eve. Her book is destined to have the most revolutionary effect on human thought since the crucifixion of Jesus. I give you this year's winner of the Nobel Prize for Literature, Paula Twitty"

The crowd roared and sirens rent the air. Paula felt someone touch her arm. It was Dippy Danny, leaning on his old golf bag, which he used as a duffle bag but which had one battered golf club sticking out of the top.

"What's happening, Danny?" Paula asked him.

"Riot in Lafayette Park," he said, and grinned. He must have been in his fifties, but his face was smooth, like a boy's. He never needed a shave. Paula looked around and saw her friends rushing in the direction of Lafayette Park.

"Come on, Dippy!" someone shouted.

"Hell no, I won't go!" Danny shouted back.

"What are they rioting about?" Paul said.

"They don't have anything to eat," Danny said. "I say, let them eat cake."

"You bum!" A burly policeman they called Judge to his face and Marquis de Sade to his back spun Danny around to face him. "Don't you care about the little children sleeping on grates in the streets?"

"That was uncalled for, Judge," Danny said. "If they don't want to sleep in the streets, let them go out and get a job."

"I ought to bust you one," the policeman said, "but I never could hit a kid. What are you smirking at, Twitty?"

"I was thinking how well you worded that, Judge," Paula said, shrinking back out of hitting range and stumbling on some steps.

"We are here on the steps of the Lincoln Memorial for the inauguration of the first President of the United States in the 21st century," Dan Rather said, "And it is a historic occasion indeed, for today we will witness the swearing-in of the first —."

Paula leaned back against the seat of her plush limousine, watching Dan on television, and thought about how hard she had worked for this day. "President Dennis Hastert, who has held our government together for the last six months since the unsettling events that put him in office, is leaving the White House with the First Lady in his limousine," Dan said. "He assumed office after President Bill Clinton was impeached and eloped with former Pentagon employee Linda Tripp, leaving behind the historic note that reads, 'I cannot govern without the woman I love by my side'; and Vice President Al Gore resigned to join a Buddhist monastery."

Paula reflected on the further losses the country had sustained since then. Dan Quayle, the Republican presidential nominee, disappeared after returning from a visit to Iraq to inspect Saddam Hussein's chemical weapons without wearing a gas mask; and Reform Party candidate

146   *Beneath the Rain Shadow*

Ross Perot renounced his American citizenship after he bought Mexico. The parties rushed to fill their vacancies, but burning crosses, marches by armed militiamen, and church bombings so revolted the American public that they swept the Democratic candidate in by a vote of five to one.

The traffic on Pennsylvania Avenue was fierce. Paula's driver looked at her apologetically, and she smiled at him, cool on the outside as always, but inside raging with visions of the brave new world of justice and equality that she would help to build.

"The traffic on Pennsylvania Avenue is fierce," Dan Rather said, "but dignitaries are arriving and taking their places on the steps of the memorial. This will be the first inauguration in American history where everybody will stand. The President-elect will take the oath of office just below the brooding statue of Abraham Lincoln, the Great Emancipator. To my right is former Congresswoman Patricia Schroeder, rumored to be the next Secretary of Defense. I've just caught sight of Ralph Nader, who will head the new Department of Consumer Affairs."

As her driver turned into the entrance of the memorial, Paula felt ready for the historic role she was about to play.

"The President-elect's car has arrived," Dan Rather said. "The Secret Service is all over the place." A tremendous cheer went up in the crowd, and the Marine Band got set to play "Hail to the Chief" as soon as the new President took the oath of office. Tears were running down Dan Rather's face as he said, "President-elect and Mrs. Jesse Jackson have stepped out of their car and are coming up the steps. Behind them, ready to swear in the new President, is the Chief Justice of the United States, the Honorable Paula Twitty."

Best Friends

rystal and Suzanne had called Charlie "our boyfriend" since the third grade at Broad View Elementary in Oak Harbor. People wondered how they stayed best friends and dated the same boy all through high school. Charlie called Crystal and Suzanne "my girlfriends," and when people looked incredulous, he would say, "I am too beautiful for one woman alone."

They had shared him good-naturedly for the most part, scrupulously taking turns going with him to big events, but now the crunch had come. Who would he take to the senior prom? This was not an event that could depend on whose turn it was. This was the Diamond Jubilee of High School, the crowning moment of that part of their lives.

Crystal and Suzanne could not have been more different. Crystal was one of only three girls in the physics class. She headed the Odyssey of the Mind teams all through high school, and she had been accepted into the MIT biophysics program. Her burning ambition was to invent a biochemical process that would neutralize plutonium, and her computer contained four years of research on everything scientists had so far discovered about plutonium.

Suzanne won all the home economics prizes, was president of her 4-H club, the Happy Homemakers, and had been accepted into Western Washington University's Home Economics program. She planned to specialize in interior design so that she would have a profession to fall back on and support the two children she planned to have, in case anything happened to her husband, whom she pictured as being a corporation executive on the CEO track.

Charlie had a football scholarship to Texas A&M. He loved Crystal and Suzanne, but already thought of them as friends of his youth, to whom he and his wife (preferably a granddaughter of Ross Perot, but failing that, an oil

148   *Beneath the Rain Shadow*

millionaire's daughter) would always send Christmas cards.

Crystal sat at her computer working on an article for *Scientific American* while Suzanne bounced on Crystal's bed.

"I couldn't sleep last night thinking about the prom," Suzanne said. "I got so exasperated, I finally thought, 'Why don't we let Charlie choose?' "

They looked at each other a moment then said, in unison, "Nah!"

"Well he couldn't," Crystal said. "He's not equipped. We can't put a burden like that on such a fragile mind."

"It would break his heart," Suzanne agreed.

"I think he should take you," Crystal said. "In 30 years I'll have the Nobel Prize for Physics and the Medal of Freedom, but nobody will have even heard of you. I don't need this as much as you do."

Suzanne smiled. "I think you should go with him," she said. "I can go with any other boy I want, but who else would take you? I don't want to deprive you of the last date you'll probably ever have."

Crystal smiled wider. "Let's let the laws of probability decide. Long straw gets Charlie."

Crystal prepared the straws, and Suzanne drew the short one.

"Probability's will be done," Crystal said, and smirked.

When Crystal went to the bathroom, Suzanne found the long straw under a pillow and knew Crystal had been holding two short ones when she offered them to Suzanne for drawing. "You're the last straw," she said to the straw.

She slipped a computer disk out of her purse, put it into Crystal's floppy drive, and tapped a few keys.

Crystal came back to an empty room. In place of the mathematical equations showing on her computer 10 minutes ago, the words "delete *.*" were blinking on and off all over the screen in 36 colors.

ε❧